# American Inside Out

## Workbook

## Upper Intermediate

MACMILLAN

Published by Macmillan Education
Between Towns Road, Oxford OX4 3PP
A division of Macmillan Publishers Limited
Companies and representatives throughout the world.
© Macmillan Publishers Limited, 2003

ISBN 1405002905

Text © Philip Kerr, Sue Kay and Vaughan Jones 2001
Design and illustration © Macmillan Publishers Limited 2001

First published 2001
American Edition 2003

Project management by Desmond O'Sullivan, ELT Publishing Services.
Edited by Alyson Maskell, Phoenix Publishing Services.
Designed by Jackie Hill at 320 Design.
Illustrated by Martin Chatterton pp. 4, 8, 18, 19, 20, 27, 30;
Julian Mosedale p. 12; Nicola Slater pp. 16, 31
Cover design by Andrew Oliver.
Cover painting In Coconut Grove © Howard Hodgkin.

The authors and publishers would like to thank the following for permission to
reproduce copyright material:
**Excerpt** from *Angela's Ashes* by Frank McCourt (HarperCollins Publishers Ltd.,
1996), © Frank McCourt 1996, reprinted by permission of the publisher.
**Excerpts** from "Bollywood Superstar's Marriage Shocks Fans" by Amit Roy
and Rahul Bed published in *Daily Telegraph* 11/13/99; "Rich Pickings for a
Wronged Wife" by Caroline Davies published in *Daily Telegraph* 1/16/99, both
© Telegraph Group 1999; "My Marriage is for Life, Insists Hillary" by Toby
Harnden published in *Daily Telegraph* 1/20/00 and "Couples Cash in by Taking
Classes in Marriage" by Phillip Delves Broughton published in *Daily Telegraph*
4/25/00, both © Telegraph Group 2000, all reprinted by permission of
Telegraph Group Limited.
**Excerpt** from *The Best Book of Urban Myths Ever* by Yorick Brown and Mike
Flynn (Carlton Books, 1998), reprinted by permission of the publisher.
**Excerpts** from *Collins Cobuild English Dictionary for Advanced Learners*
(HarperCollins Publishers Ltd., 2001), © HarperCollins Ltd. 2001, Updated from
the Bank of English. Based on the Cobuild series, developed in collaboration
with the University of Birmingham, reprinted by permission of the publishers.

Although every effort has been made to contact copyright holders before
publication, this has not always been possible. If notified, the publisher
undertakes to rectify any errors or omissions at the earliest opportunity.

The authors and publishers would like to thank the following for permission to
reproduce their photographs: Corbis/Reed Kaestner p. 36, Photex p. 34 (h),
Roger Ressmeyer p. 34 (g), Brian Vikander p. 34 (f); *Angela's Ashes* © Angelus
Films/Ronald Grant Cinema Archive p. 11, Matilda Columbia Tristar Films
(UK)/Ronald Grant Cinema Archive p. 11, *Addam's Family* Columbia Tristar
Films/Ronald Grant Cinema Archive p. 11; Rex p. 6, Rex/N.A.S.A. p. 34 (b),
Rex/SIPA p. 34 (c); Stone pp. 34 (a, d, e).

The illustrations on p. 9 are from *Happy Families* by Steven Appleby, published
by Bloomsbury Publishing Plc.

Printed and bound in Thailand
2007  2006  2005  2004  2003
10  9  8  7  6  5  4  3  2

# Contents

# 1 *Images*

## Images, Pictures, and Paintings

**1** Complete each sentence with *image, picture,* or *painting*.

a) He tried to cultivate a sophisticated _____ , but it didn't work.

b) It's amazing—she's the mirror _____ of her mother.

c) British _____ is not very well known internationally.

d) Excuse me, would you mind taking my _____ ?

e) After three weeks at the health spa, he was a _____ of health.

f) There was a large oil _____ by Turner at the entrance to the gallery.

**2** Complete each quotation by matching a phrase from box A with a phrase from box B.

A

a) A celebrity is a person who works hard all his life to become well known, then wears dark glasses to

b) A celebrity is any well-known TV or movie star who looks

c) Fashion is a form of ugliness so intolerable that we have to

d) In the future, everyone will

e) Some are born great, some achieve greatness, and some

f) To be a celebrity in America is to

B

1 alter it every six months. (Oscar Wilde)
2 avoid being recognized. (Fred Allen)
3 be famous for fifteen minutes. (Andy Warhol)
4 be forgiven everything. (Mary McGrory)
5 hire public relations officers. (Daniel Boorstin)
6 like he spends more than two hours working on his hair. (Steve Martin)

## Grammar

**1** Circle the most appropriate verb forms in the text below.

I (a) *am just buying / just bought / will just buy* this really cool pair of blue sunglasses. I (b) *am walking/ walked / was walking* around a flea market when I (c) *have seen / saw / see* this new designer boutique. I (d) *had been looking / used to look / would look* for the right style for ages, and there they were. I (e) *have just had / was just having / just had* to get them. I (f) *am going / have gone / have been going* to a club next Wednesday—nobody ever (g) *is going / goes / went* to that club on the weekend— and these shades (h) *have been / had been / will be* perfect, you know what I mean? Everyone (i) *has worn / is wearing / would wear* them these days. They're so cool!

**2** Four of the sentences below contain an auxiliary verb (*do, does, did, has, have, was, were*) that should not be there. Cross it out.

a) Do you know anybody who has been in prison?

b) Does anyone in your family does speak English fluently?

c) Have you ever done anything that you did not mean to do?

d) How long have you known your closest friend?

e) Is there anybody in your family who does wears a fur coat?

f) What were you doing before you started this exercise?

g) When was the last time you have read your horoscope?

h) Who were you were speaking to last night?

**3** In four of the sentences below, an auxiliary verb (*do, does, did, has, have, was, were*) is missing. Insert the missing auxiliaries.

a) Do you realize I gotten tired of telling you?

b) Did I tell you about who we met last night?

c) Have you finished that book I lent you?

d) Haven't we met before somewhere?

e) Where were you when you needed?

f) Who did you say you going out with?

g) Who stole the cookie from the cookie jar?

h) Why you not tell me you were married?

**4** Complete each pair of sentences by choosing *So* or *Neither* and filling in the blank with an auxiliary verb. Three of the pairs of sentences are completely untrue. Which ones are they?

a) Berlin holds an annual film festival.
   So/Neither _____ Venice.

b) *Star Wars* is one of the most successful movies of all time.
   So/Neither _____ *The Jungle Book*.

c) Nicolas Cage has never won an Oscar.
   So/Neither _____ Jodie Foster.

d) The director of *Titanic* won an Oscar in 1997.
   So/Neither _____ Jack Nicholson.

e) Isabella Rossellini has a famous father.
   So/Neither _____ Jane Fonda.

f) Sharon Stone has never gotten married.
   So/Neither _____ Richard Gere.

g) Mel Gibson was not born in America.
   So/Neither _____ Arnold Schwarzenegger.

h) Frank Sinatra was born in the 1930s.
   So/Neither _____ Michelle Pfeiffer.

**5** Use a tag to complete each phrase.

a) They have nothing in common,
   _____ ?

b) She never said she would marry him,
   _____ ?

c) O.K., I forgot to tell you yesterday, but I'm telling you now, _____ ?

d) You've been taking a nap, _____ ?

e) Somebody likes her music, _____ ?

f) She never calls you, _____ ?

g) Nobody wants to look like that,
   _____ ?

h) Let's change the subject, _____ ?

**6** Rewrite the questions below, using the sentence beginnings.

a) What is your biggest secret?
   I'd like to know _____
   _____
   _____

b) When did you have your first kiss?
   I was wondering _____
   _____
   _____

c) Are you going out with anyone?
   I want to know _____
   _____
   _____

d) Who was the last person that you talked to?
   I was wondering _____
   _____
   _____

e) Who do you dislike the most?
   I'd like to know _____
   _____
   _____

f) Have you ever broken the law?
   Could you tell me _____
   _____
   _____

g) Do you take vitamins?
   I want to know _____
   _____
   _____

h) Could you answer these questions truthfully?
   Do you think _____
   _____
   _____

# Listening

**1**  Listen to part of a radio program. (If you don't have the recording, read the tapescript on p. 78.) Name the stars and match each one to an excerpt from the program by writing a number in the box.

> Mariah Carey   Elton John
> Michael Jackson   Prince

a) ☐                    b) ☐

name: _____

name: _____

c) ☐                    d) ☐

name: _____

name: _____

**2**  Listen again and answer the questions. Write your answers in the boxes provided. (MC – Mariah Carey; MJ – Michael Jackson; EJ – Elton John; P – Prince)

a) Who chose a weird name? ☐

b) Who couldn't see very well? ☐

c) Who enjoyed being with animals? ☐

d) Who is English? ☐

e) Who stopped working in his twenties? ☐

f) Who was a child star? ☐

g) Whose music was very forgettable? ☐

h) Which men wore women's clothes? ☐ ☐

i) Who was popular with younger children?
☐ ☐

**3** Match each word from column A with a word from column B to make a phrase you heard on the recording.

| A | | B | |
|---|---|---|---|
| a) | change | 1 | aged |
| b) | curly | 2 | awards |
| c) | cute | 3 | clips |
| d) | first | 4 | color |
| e) | middle | 5 | kid |
| f) | MTV | 6 | paper |
| g) | toilet | 7 | prize |
| h) | video | 8 | wig |

**4** Complete each phrase with a preposition from the box.

> as   at   for   in   on   of   to

a) known _____ the way they look

b) starting life _____ a pianist

c) his taste _____ glasses

d) putting _____ weight

e) _____ everyone's surprise

f) he preferred the company _____ monkeys

g) ten years old _____ the time

h) back _____ the point

i) at the age _____ 25

j) don't attempt _____ understand

k) enough _____ that

 Now listen to the recording again to check your answers to exercises 3 and 4.

# Pronunciation

 Listen to the following short dialogues. In each dialogue, write a check (✔) next to the speaker (A or B) who sounds more interested.

a) A: I just saw Warren Beatty on the street.
   B: Really?

b) A: Guess what. There's a documentary about Prince Charles on TV tonight.
   B: Another one?

c) A: Don't you think he looks just like Paul Newman?
   B: More like my dad.

d) A: Let's have a really good night out.
   B: Clubbing again?

e) A: Good luck on the test tomorrow.
   B: Thanks.

f) A: Pronunciation work?
   B: Yes, intonation.

# Vocabulary

**1** Complete the text with words from the box below. All words and expressions come from the text about Madonna in your Student Book.

> ambition detail eye image time
> resemblance talent thing platinum

He doesn't bear any (a) _____ to any pop star you've ever seen. Nor does he have any musical (b) _____ to speak of. But Kevin Scroter, from Clondalkin near Dublin, has his (c) _____ on fame and fortune. Kevin just dyed his hair (d) _____ blond and will be going for a complete change of (e) _____ as soon as his other preparations are complete. He has studied Ronan Keating, Ricky Martin, and the others down to the last (f) _____ . Kevin is determined to make it big. Kevin wants to be the new sex symbol, top of the charts, prince of our hearts. Will he achieve his burning (g) _____ ? Only (h) _____ will tell, but one (i) _____ is certain—he may keep us waiting a long time.

**2** Complete each sentence with an appropriate verb. The first letter has been provided for you.

a) How often do you g_____ clubbing?

b) I could really g_____ for a drink!

c) I wouldn't t_____ what he says at face value if I were you.

d) If I won the lottery, I wouldn't let it a_____ my way of life.

e) No, thanks. I'm trying not to p_____ on too much weight.

f) She should have gotten the job, but she didn't l_____ professional at the interview.

g) We are hoping to d_____ a good job with our research.

h) They don't seem to h_____ much in common—a real odd couple!

i) They'll probably l_____ touch with some of their friends when they move overseas.

j) When we first met, he didn't m_____ much of an impression on me.

k) You'd better just s_____ your pride and apologize.

**3** Match each phrase from box A with a phrase from box B to make a mini-dialogue.

A

> a) Do you mind if I have another chocolate?
> b) Did you hear? She had her nose pierced!
> c) I can't stand the way she looks on the latest video.
> d) I hope she doesn't show up with that new boyfriend of hers.
> e) I'm ready!
> f) I mean, what exactly were you thinking?
> g) You're not going to go out with him, are you?

B

> 1 You're kidding! She didn't!
> 2 Heaven forbid! He's a nightmare.
> 3 I guess not. But you know, he is very good-looking.
> 4 Neither can I. The music's garbage too.
> 5 Right. Let's get started.
> 6 To be honest, I'm not sure myself.
> 7 Go ahead. Help yourself!

**4** Use a dictionary to complete the chart below.

| adjective | noun | verb |
| --- | --- | --- |
| _____ | adaptation | _____ |
| ambitious | _____ | – |
| – | emergence | _____ |
| _____ | impression | _____ |
| innocent | _____ | – |
| _____ | strategy | – |
| tempting | _____ | _____ |

**5** Use a word from the chart above to complete each sentence.

a) The devil didn't _____ me! It was you!

b) Did anything interesting _____ from your conversation?

c) He took up a _____ position near the exit.

d) His burning _____ was to get a job in the bank.

e) I lost my _____ when I left home.

f) I can't come. Don't try to _____ me!

g) This company needs to _____ to the changing market conditions.

# Writing

**1** Choose the best title for the magazine article below. You will correct punctuation and capitalization later.

    a) Cheap Style   b) Looking Good and Feeling Good   c) The Cost of an Image   d) The Drug Connection

> If you walk down any street in any town anywhere, you'll see them the Levi's jeans, a Tommy Hilfiger T-shirt, Nike sneakers and, perhaps, a pair of Ray-Bans oh, don't forget the Rolex watch and possibly a scent of what might just be a Calvin Klein perfume it could be you and it could be me almost all of us, at some point in our lives, buy something because of the name that is printed on it we buy an image and we are prepared to pay for it but how many of these products are the real thing none of the big companies will admit how much they lose, but the counterfeit trade runs into billions of dollars each year on London's Oxford Street or the streets of New York, it's easy to buy fake labels for a fraction of the normal price if you're really low on cash, there's an even better way of doing it if you know the right person, you can buy a bag of fake Lacoste crocodiles sew these onto some cheap T-shirts keep a few for yourself and sell the rest to your friends does anybody care not many of us are likely to have much sympathy for the big fashion companies surely they can afford it but stop for a minute and think about where all the money goes the police now have growing evidence that much of the money goes back into drug dealing some terrorist organizations are funded by counterfeit goods and supported by profits made from the sale of fake T-shirts so, next time you're tempted by a cheap T-shirt or some other knockoff, make sure you know where your money is really going.

**2** Divide the text into four paragraphs. Choose a short title for each paragraph.

**3** Now divide the paragraphs into sentences. Insert punctuation (periods [ . ], commas [ , ], and question marks [ ? ]). Write the capital letters where they belong. Each paragraph should have the following number of sentences:

    Paragraph 1: 6       Paragraph 3: 6
    Paragraph 2: 7       Paragraph 4: 2

**4** Eleven of the twelve words below are spelled incorrectly. Correct them. You can read the text again to check your answers.

> aford   evidance   lifes   terorist
> allmost   favrite   milion   simpathy
> companys   freinds   parfume   scent

**5** You are going to write about a famous living person that you like or admire. You should use the paragraph outline opposite to help you.

*Paragraph 1*
Who is he/she? Age? What is he/she famous for? How popular is he/she in your country?

*Paragraph 2*
What does he/she look like? Has he/she ever changed his/her appearance or image? Do you know what he/she has been doing recently? What is the best thing he/she has ever done?

*Paragraph 3*
When did you first become aware of him/her? Have you ever seen him/her in person? How long have you been a fan? What do you particularly like about him/her? Is there anything you don't like about him/her?

You should write approximately 180 words.

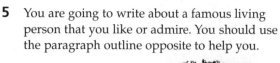

*A singer/musician? A movie star? A professional athlete? A politician? Someone else?*

# 2 Family

## The Right Family

We're staying together for the sake of the children.

You're ruining our lives!

Well, you ruined mine!

As soon as I was old enough to become an individual you didn't like me!

That's not true!

Actually, we NEVER liked you.

## Grammar

**1** Rewrite the second sentence, beginning with the words given, so that it means the same as the first.

a) They didn't have enough money to buy me lots of new clothes.

They couldn't afford _____

_____

b) They would never let me forget to do my homework.

They always reminded _____

_____

c) They told me that it was a good idea to go to church every week.

They encouraged _____

_____

d) They always refused to allow me to bring friends home.

They never let _____

_____

e) They insisted on me coming home at ten o'clock every night.

They made _____

_____

f) They said that night clubs were dangerous places and that I shouldn't go to them.

They warned _____

_____

g) It was my father's intention that I should work in his factory.

My father expected _____

_____

h) I learned from my parents about respecting authority.

My parents taught _____

_____

i) They had hoped that I would be like them.

They would have liked _____

_____

j) I succeeded in running away from home when I was 14.

I managed _____

_____

**2** Circle the correct form of each verb.

a) It's amazing how she avoids *to do* / *doing* the housework every day.

b) Has she ever offered *to help* / *helping* with the cooking?

c) We'd prefer her *to do* / *doing* some of the housework sometimes.

d) Maybe we should pay her *to clean* / *cleaning* her room.

e) How much time can a girl waste *to look* / *looking* in the mirror?

f) Do you think she would ever consider *to be* / *being* helpful around the house?

→

g) How long do you think it will be before she has finished *to get / getting* dressed?

h) We don't mind her *to come / coming* back home late now and then.

i) Anyway, she tends *to come / coming* home on the back of her boyfriend's motorcycle.

**3** Complete the text with a suitable preposition.

In June of last year I had my final school exams, so in May I was really concentrating (a) _____ studying. My parents insisted (b) _____ me staying in to study every night, but I didn't need them to tell me what to do. However, that month I met a guy I really liked who invited me out. I knew my parents would disapprove (c) _____ him because he was a different religion. I thought they would try to prevent me (d) _____ seeing him. Anyway, I didn't think they would object (e) _____ me going round to see a friend one evening, and I didn't tell them I was actually going to a party. I was really looking forward (f) _____ the big night. But when I got home from the party, my parents were waiting. They said they had been very worried (g) _____ me, and they accused me (h) _____ lying to them. Apparently, the friend I was supposed to be visiting had called during the evening and asked to speak to me. If I had known that she liked the same guy, I would've known not to depend (i) _____ her! When we talked about it, she wouldn't apologize (j) _____ what she had done and blamed me (k) _____ taking Michael away from her. I failed my exams.

**4** Complete the text with words from the box.

> afraid  allergic  angry  covered  essential
> fond  hopeless  interested  proud  used

Two years ago I went to a language school in Texas and stayed with a host family. At the time, I was (a) _____ at English and couldn't understand them very well, but I could see they were more than a little strange. They got (b) _____ with me when I arrived because I didn't take my shoes off. They were really (c) _____ of their house and (d) _____ of getting even a little bit of dirt on their carpet. But my first big problem was in the bedroom. I am (e) _____ to cats,

and there, sitting on the bed, which was (f) _____ in cat hair, was the ugliest animal you have ever seen. "He always sleeps here," they said. "You'll soon get (g) _____ to him." I explained that I wasn't very (h) _____ of animals, but they didn't seem to be the least bit (i) _____ in what I said. The next day, I called the housing office and said that it was (j) _____ for me to find a different family to live with.

**5** Each of the sentences below contains a word that should not be there. Cross it out.

a) He didn't want that his friends to find out about his father's job.

b) His father made him to join the act.

c) I've considered of buying my own apartment, but I can't afford to.

d) We'd want for them to do well in school.

e) I look forward to be hearing from you.

f) Gina's mom manages her to stay in shape.

g) My father taught for me to swim when I was five.

h) We'd warn them about not to take drugs.

i) I never waste time at ironing my clothes.

j) They let her to have what she wants all the time.

k) We can't afford us to stay at an expensive hotel.

l) We are tend to work late.

# Pronunciation

Put the words in the box into seven groups according to the underlined vowel sounds.

> off  look  black  bought  son  can't
> could  register  next  knock  happen
> head  father  daughter  stick  flood
> middle  shopping  thin  hug

/ɪ/ did _____

/ɛ/ bet _____

/æ/ cat _____

/ɑ/ not _____

/ɔ/ saw _____

/ʊ/ good _____

/ʌ/ but _____

🔊 Listen to the recording to check your answers. Practice saying the words.

# Reading

**1** Read this excerpt of a very well-known book. Which of the pictures below comes from the movie of this book?

a)

b)

c)

(from *Angela's Ashes* by Frank McCourt)

My father and mother should have stayed in New York where they met and married and where I was born. Instead, they returned to Ireland when I was four; my brother, Malachy, three; the twins, Oliver and Eugene, barely one; and my sister, Margaret, dead and gone.

When I look back on my childhood, I wonder how I survived at all. It was, of course, a miserable childhood; the happy childhood is hardly worth your while. Worse than the ordinary miserable childhood is the miserable Irish childhood, and worse yet is the miserable Irish Catholic childhood.

People everywhere brag and whimper about the woes of their early years, but nothing can compare with the Irish version: the poverty; the shiftless, loquacious alcoholic father; the pious, defeated mother moaning by the fire; pompous priests; bullying schoolmasters; the English and the terrible things they did to us for eight hundred long years. [...]

My father, Malachy McCourt, was born on a farm in Toome, County Antrim. Like his father before, he grew up wild, in trouble with the English, or the Irish, or both. He fought with the old IRA and for some desperate act he wound up a fugitive with a price on his head.

When I was a child I would look at my father, the thinning hair, the collapsing teeth, and wonder why anyone would give money for a head like that. When I was thirteen my father's mother told me a secret: as a wee lad your poor father was dropped on his head. It was an accident, he was never the same after, and you must remember that people dropped on their heads can be a bit peculiar.

**2** Read the text again. Decide if each of the following statements is true (T) or false (F).

a) Frank (the author) grew up in New York.
b) His parents grew up in New York.
c) He went to Ireland with his five brothers and sisters.
d) He came from a poor family.
e) He did not like his teachers at school.
f) Ireland was the best country to grow up in.
g) His father was never in trouble.
h) His father was not an attractive man.
i) His paternal grandmother died before he was born.
j) His father's accident affected his life.

**3** Complete each sentence below with a word from the box.

| at | for | in | like | of | on | to | with |
|----|-----|----|----|----|----|----|------|

a) I look back _____ my childhood with great pleasure.
b) She doesn't really like him _____ all.
c) _____ course I don't want to marry you!
d) There's nothing that can compare _____ a romantic walk along a beach.
e) What exactly did they do _____ you to make you so scared?
f) In many ways, she is just _____ her parents—unfortunately!
g) She was always _____ trouble with her teachers.
h) I'd give a lot of money _____ a chance like that.

Now read the text again to check your answers.

**4** Find a word or phrase in the text that matches the definitions below.

a) problems or difficulties
b) talkative
c) ended up as
d) person running away from the police
e) young boy
f) strange; weird

# Vocabulary

**1** Complete the chart with adjectives that match the nouns on the left.

| nouns | adjectives |
|---|---|
| allergy | a) _____ |
| compatibility | b) _____ |
| embarrassment | c) _____ |
| fondness | d) _____ |
| humiliation | e) _____ |
| impatience | f) _____ |
| dependence | g) _____ |

**2** Now complete each sentence with either a noun or an adjective from the chart above.

a) He suffers from a serious _____ to cigarette smoke.

b) His _____ on his parents will have to end when he leaves home.

c) I'm very _____ of you, but I don't want to go out with you.

d) The Dallas Cowboys were totally _____ in the final, losing by 17 points to the New York Giants.

e) The behavior of the fans was a serious _____ to the government.

f) Some couples have blood tests to see if they are _____ .

g) The students were _____ for the term to end.

**3** Match a word from column A with a word from column B to make a common combination. Then use the combinations to complete the sentences below.

| A | B |
|---|---|
| job | background |
| country | class |
| family | cottage |
| academic | lunch |
| social | manners |
| Sunday | prospects |
| table | qualifications |

a) Advertisers think carefully about _____ _____ when selling their products.

b) He had _____ _____ like a pig.

c) He'll need a _____ _____ to get a better job.

d) Americans often eat _____ _____ instead of breakfast and lunch.

e) They both came from a _____ _____ of poverty and violence.

f) We rented a _____ _____ for the summer.

g) With the high unemployment rate here, my _____ _____ are very low.

**4** Put this story in the correct order.

1 [a]  2 [ ]  3 [ ]  4 [ ]
5 [ ]  6 [ ]  7 [ ]  8 [ ]
9 [ ]  10 [ ]  11 [ ]

a) Most of my friends tend to go
b) along better with small, quiet types. I used to go
c) out with a real Adonis type, but I broke
d) up with him when I caught him fooling
e) to deny it when I accused him of it. I got so fed
f) over him soon, and now I've given
g) for tall, dark men, but I seem to get
h) up with his lies, and I never knew what he was
i) up to. But I got
j) around with my friends. He even tried
k) up even looking at men like that.

**5** Look at the following example.

New word: *lace*
Translation: _____
Grammatical information: noncountable noun
Combinations: Irish lace, necklace
Example: The tablecloth was edged with lace.

Find eight more new words from this unit. Use a dictionary to help you write similar information for the new words.

# Writing

**1** Complete the letters below with the phrases that are given.

---

Dear Mr. Hayabashi,

I am writing with reference to your visit to Chicago on the 19th of this month. (1) _d_ that (2) ____ to meet you in person at the airport when you arrive. (3) ____ for which I must apologize.

However, my colleague, Susan Fleming, the director of sales and marketing, (4) ____ in the international arrivals area and to accompany you to your hotel. (5) ____

I hope that you will excuse this inconvenience, but I am sure that you will be well taken care of by Ms. Fleming. She has arranged a full schedule of entertainment for the evening, (6) ____

(7) ____ May I take this opportunity to wish you a pleasant flight. I hope that your stay in Chicago is both enjoyable and profitable.

Yours sincerely,

*Peter Sullivan*

---

Dear Patty,

How are things? Are you still planning to come and stay with us later this month? I'm really looking forward to seeing you again and catching up on all your news.

Anyway, the reason I'm writing is that (8) ____ , so (9) ____ to come to the airport to meet you. (10) ____ about that.

Don't worry, though. Robyn, one of the people I share an apartment with, said that she (11) ____ . She'll be waiting for you when you come through the arrivals gate. She has long blond hair and she'll be carrying a red umbrella. (12) ____

I won't get back from my business trip until the next morning, but Robyn will take care of you. She has tickets for the Radiohead concert, (13) ____

(14) ____
Love,
Mindy

---

a) 'll come to the airport to pick you up

b) but if you don't want to do that, she'll go along with whatever you want to do.

c) I look forward to seeing you again at our meeting on the 20th.

d) I sincerely regret

e) I will be unable

f) I won't be able

g) I'm really sorry

h) See you on Tuesday morning!

i) She will be holding a sign with your name.

j) She has a picture of you, so she knows what you look like.

k) should you wish to avail yourself of the opportunity.

l) something has come up with my job

m) This is due to unforeseen and unavoidable work commitments

n) will be there to welcome you

**2** Shortly after receiving these letters, Mr. Hayabashi and Patty learned that the time of their flight had been changed. The plane will now arrive in Chicago at 5 P.M., three hours earlier than planned.

Look at the phrases below and write H if they come from Mr Hayabashi's reply or P if they come from Patty's reply.

a) All your old friends send their love.

b) I am sorry to hear that other duties require your attention.

c) I have received your letter concerning my arrival in London.

d) I hope that she will not be inconvenienced by the adjustments to my schedule.

e) I hope that this will be O.K.

f) I would be grateful if you would confirm the new arrangements.

g) Is your new boss giving you grief?

h) Thanks for your letter about meeting me at the airport.

i) Will she be able to make it at this time?

j) Your former colleagues send their best wishes.

**3** Now write two short letters, one from Mr. Hayabashi to Peter Sullivan, and one from Patty to Mindy. In the letters, explain the change in arrival time and apologize for any inconvenience.

# 3 Money

## Money Songs

Complete the song lyrics in box A with the phrases from box B.

A

| | |
|---|---|
| a) | Money, money, money, must be funny |
| b) | I don't care too much for money |
| c) | Money for nothing |
| d) | Money, it's a crime |
| e) | Money's too tight to mention |

B

| | |
|---|---|
| 1 | and chicks for free (Dire Straits) |
| 2 | 'cause money can't buy me love (The Beatles) |
| 3 | I can't even qualify for my pension (Simply Red) |
| 4 | in the rich man's world (Abba) |
| 5 | share it fairly but don't take a slice of my pie (Pink Floyd) |

## Grammar

**1** Put the words and phrases below into the correct column.

| | | | |
|---|---|---|---|
| Argentina | Atlantic | Caribbean | China |
| Gulf of Mexico | India | Middle East | |
| Gobi Desert | Andes | Lake Superior | Mecca |
| moon | Mount Everest | Amazon River | |
| Africa | Texas | European Union | Venus |

**with the**                    **without the**

_____          _____
_____          _____
_____          _____
_____          _____
_____          _____
_____          _____
_____          _____
_____          _____
_____          _____

**2** Look at the following quotations. Some of them have one or more definite articles that should not be there. Cross out the articles that should not be there.

a) The credit cards are what the people use after they discover that money can't buy everything. (anon.)

b) The empty pockets make the empty heads. (William Carlos Williams)

c) The life is short, and so is the money. (Bertolt Brecht)

d) The money can't buy the friends, but you can get a better class of enemy. (Spike Milligan)

e) The money is better than the poverty, if only for the financial reasons. (Woody Allen)

f) The money isn't everything. There are also the credit cards and the traveler's checks. (anon.)

g) The poor have more children, but the rich have more relatives. (anon.)

**3** Fill in each blank with *a, an,* or *the.*

(a) _____ rich man was driving down (b) _____ street in (c) _____ center of town when (d) _____ truck crashed into his car. It was (e) _____ serious accident: (f) _____ driver's side of (g) _____ car was completely destroyed and (h) _____ man's arm was cut off in (i) _____ accident. A few minutes later, (j) _____ police officer arrived at (k) _____ scene and found (l) _____ driver, who was shouting, "My car! My car!" (m) _____ police officer looked at him and said gently, "Sir, I think you should be more concerned about your arm than (n) _____ car." (o) _____ driver looked down at where his arm should have been and screamed, "My Rolex! My Rolex!"

**4** Fill in each blank with *a, an, the,* or – (no article).

If you were seriously rich, what would you do with all (a) _____ money? For (b) _____ start, you might like to buy (c) _____ island where you could go on (d) _____ vacation. D'Arros, (e) _____ small island in (f) _____ Seychelles, would cost about $20 million, and for this you would get (g) _____ private beach, (h) _____ airstrip, and (i) _____ three homes. You would, of course, need some kind of (j) _____ transportation. (k) _____ most expensive jet you can buy is the *Gulfstream V*. (l) _____ regular price is $35 million, but if you are prepared to spend (m) _____ extra $5 million, you could get (n) _____ variety of (o) _____ special features. For your vacation pictures, you could buy (p) _____ camera for $60,000. This antique camera was originally made in 1901, and all (q) _____ metal components of (r) _____ camera are made of (s) _____ solid gold. This may all sound like (t) _____ dream, but (u) _____ all you need is (v) _____ rich partner. When Soraya Khashoggi divorced her husband, Adnan, (w) _____ Saudi businessman, (x) _____ divorce settlement was over $900 million.

**5** Correct the mistake in each of these sentences.

a) If you are the president of your country, what would you do about the environment?

b) If I did ever had the chance, I'd take a year off and travel.

c) If I could live anywhere in the world, I'd probably bought a beach villa in Tahiti.

d) If I didn't need to learn English for my job, I would stop a long time ago.

e) If I didn't come to school yesterday, I would have stayed home.

f) If I knew this was going to be so difficult, I would never have started it.

g) If I was exercising more when I was younger, I would be in better shape now.

h) If I was born with very rich parents, I wouldn't be working at this job, would I?

**6** Match the *if* clauses (a–h) with the correct main clauses (1–8).

a) If you could spare a few minutes,
b) If you hadn't been so intent on getting rich,
c) If you hadn't taken a few risks,
d) If you had saved money like me,
e) If you had studied a little more,
f) If you just had taken a shot at it,
g) If you weren't so absent-minded,
h) If you weren't so intelligent,

1 you wouldn't have seen the need in the market.
2 you wouldn't have made your fortune.
3 you might have found a lot more happiness.
4 would you help me?
5 you would find the exam a lot easier.
6 you wouldn't have lost it.
7 you might enjoy it.
8 you would be able to afford it.

**7** Make one conditional sentence with *if* by joining each pair of sentences.

*Example*
I didn't know you were coming. That's why I didn't give you a ride.
*If I'd known you were coming, I would have given you a ride.*

a) I didn't know you were broke. Otherwise, I would've offered to pay.

_____
_____

b) It's not made of real gold. It's not worth a lot.

_____
_____

c) They cornered the market. So they raised the price.

_____
_____

d) He has a talent for spotting a golden opportunity. He has made millions.

_____
_____
_____

e) She didn't realize it was valuable. She gave it away.

_____
_____

f) My time is so precious. That's why I didn't speak to them.

_____
_____

g) My advice is this. Get a job!

_____
_____

## Listening

**1** 🔲 Listen to this excerpt from a TV quiz show. (If you don't have the recording, read the tapescript on p. 78.) Match the game contestants to the information about them.

| **job** | **home** |
| --- | --- |
| baker | Chicago |
| bank teller | Los Angeles |
| Burger Whiz manager | Toronto |

a) Margaret _____ _____

b) Germaine _baker_ _____

c) Claire _____ _____

**2** 🔲 In column A, write down the letters that the contestants choose. In column B, write down the words that they use to illustrate the letters.

| A | B |
| --- | --- |
| D | doughnut |
| | |
| | |
| | |
| | |
| | |
| | |
| | |

**3** 🔲 How much money does each contestant win?

| Margaret | Germaine | Claire |
| --- | --- | --- |
| _____ | _$400_ | _____ |
| _____ | _____ | _____ |
| Total: | Total: | Total: |
| _$1300_ | _____ | _____ |

**4** 🔲 What is the mystery phrase?

_____

**5** 🔲 Complete each phrase from the quiz show with a word from the box.

> wild   buzzer   hands   stake   struck

a) Put your _____ together.

b) There's a lot at _____ .

c) Fingers on the _____ .

d) You really _____ gold!

e) It was just a _____ guess.

**6** 🔲 Listen again (or read the tapescript) and find colloquial phrases that mean the same as those below.

a) prizes       g _ _ _ _ _ _

b) start        g _ _  t _ _ _ _ _
                r _ _ _ _ _

c) try again    t _ _ _  a _ _ _ _ _
                s _ _ _  a _  i _

d) dollars      b _ _ _ _

e) no good      n _ _ _ _ _ _  d _ _ _ _

f) good luck    c _ _ _ _  y _ _ _
                f _ _ _ _ _

g) try your luck  g _  f _ _  i _

# Vocabulary

**1** Circle the best answer: a), b), c), or d).

1 A lot of firms raise _____ by issuing new shares.
   a) capital   b) gold   c) profits   d) stock

2 Her collection of antiques is worth a _____ .
   a) chance   b) fortune   c) money
   d) wealth

3 In many families, the woman is now the main _____ .
   a) breadbasket   b) breadwinner   c) earn
   d) entrepreneur

4 It's always a good idea to save up for a _____ day.
   a) broke   b) poor   c) rainy   d) wet

5 Many _____ metals are mined in Africa.
   a) precious   b) real   c) rich   d) silver

6 Most people need a _____ when they buy a house.
   a) borrow   b) lend   c) mortgage
   d) wealth

7 The _____ offered the staff a bonus at the end of the year.
   a) company   b) employees   c) enterprise
   d) society

8 Why did you go and _____ all your money on that sports car?
   a) throw   b) blow   c) earn   d) splurge

**2** Fill in each blank with an appropriate form of a verb in the box.

| cause | have | make | set | take | give |
|-------|------|------|-----|------|------|

I called you here because your sales figures last month were appalling. Some of you need to (a) _____ some serious thought to the way you work. Our best sales people have (b) _____ a fortune in the last few weeks, but you lot have not (c) _____ advantage of the atmosphere of fear that has been (d) _____ by the recent rise in crime. No sane person wants to (e) _____ the risk of losing everything, and the public knows that our insurance policies (f) _____ sense. If you (g) _____ no idea how to sell our products, you're in the wrong job. If you (h) _____ a mess of things again and can't match the high standards (i) _____ by your co-workers, you won't have a future with this company. So, go out there, (j) _____ a stir in the company, (k) _____ some money—or find another job. Go! Sell, sell, sell!

**3** Complete each sentence with a word that begins with the letter given.

a) A f_____ of cheap imports brought down the price very quickly.

b) He spent two years d_____ from job to job before finding out what he wanted to do.

c) Her speech certainly gave us a lot of f_____ for thought.

d) I'd like to have a little more time to m_____ over your ideas.

e) I've never heard such an impractical, half-b_____ idea.

f) There was a s_____ of blood running down his face.

g) We couldn't d_____ all the information in the time we had.

**4** Complete each sentence with an appropriate form of the word in parentheses.

a) Hundreds of miners arrived in the town, but only a _____ ever became rich. (hand)

b) How much money do you need to find _____ ? (happy)

c) It was only much later that the _____ of his statement became clear. (signify)

d) Many of the immigrants had come to escape religious _____ . (persecute)

e) Some of the department heads were not convinced of the _____ of the investment. (wise)

f) The enemy will certainly try to _____ on our mistakes. (capital)

g) The farm could no longer operate _____ and was closed down. (profit)

h) I can't accept your invitation because I have an _____ with my dentist that same day. (appoint)

i) We apologize for the late _____ of Flight 378 from Kansas City. (arrive)

j) Please do not leave _____ objects unattended. (value)

# Writing

**1** The sentences opposite refer to the cartoon story. Circle the best linking word for each sentence. Sometimes more than one linking word is possible.

a) *By the time / During / Until* he was forty, he had made an enormous fortune.

b) One day, *after / as / during* he was sitting in his office, his assistant told him there was a strange man on the phone.

c) *As soon as / Just as / When* he put the phone down, he went straight to the safe.

d) He continued taking cash out of the safe *as soon as / until / while* it was empty.

e) *Then / When / While* he was ready, he took the bag and set off for the rendezvous.

f) *After / As / Until* he was leaving, he told his assistant that he had to go to the bank.

g) He kept looking over his shoulder *as soon as / as / while* he was walking down the street.

h) *During / Just as / When* the walk to the meeting place, he thought about what might have happened to his daughter.

i) *After / Just as / When* he was about to hand over the money, he recognized his daughter.

j) *Then / When / While* he thought he also recognized the man.

**2** Complete each sentence in an appropriate way.

a) Just as the businessman was about to go home for the day, _____

_____

b) During the phone conversation, the businessman _____

_____

c) While the young man was calling the businessman, his daughter _____

_____

d) When he put the phone down, the young man _____

e) The young man never thought he would ever be rich until _____

_____

f) By the time the businessman arrived at the meeting place, the young man _____

_____

g) As soon as he recognized the young man, the businessman _____

_____

**3**  Complete the following sentences with information about the story.

    a)  The first thing he did when _____ _____ was to _____
        _____

    b)  He was about to _____
        when _____

    c)  He spent the next few minutes _____
        _____

    d)  It had never crossed his mind that _____
        _____

    e)  If he hadn't _____ , he wouldn't _____

**4**  Look at the picture below, which is the next episode in the story. Think about possible answers to the questions below.

- How had the businessman made his money?
- What was the relationship between the businessman and his daughter?
- Who was the young man with a gun?
- Why did he need the money?
- What was the relationship between the girl and the young man?
- Had the businessman seen the young man before? When?
- Who killed the young man?
- What happened next?

**5**  Now write the story in your own words. You should write approximately 180 words.

# Pronunciation

**1**  🔲 Listen to the first syllable in each of the following words from this unit.

acquire  adapt  advantage  arrival  collapse compose  conditions  conservative  facilities possessions  propose  supply

None of these syllables are stressed. All of them are pronounced /ə/. Practice saying these words after the recording.

**2**  🔲 If the first, unstressed syllable is written with the letter "e," it is often pronounced /ɪ/. Listen to these words from the unit and repeat after the recording.

declare  depart  descend destroy  religious  remind

**3**  Underline the unstressed schwa sounds /ə/ in the following phrases.

    a)  a few weeks
    b)  as soon as they come
    c)  food for thought
    d)  it won't matter to me
    e)  make a mess of it
    f)  the click of a camera

🔲 Listen to the recording and repeat the phrases. Concentrate on the rhythm.

**4**  🔲 Listen to the pronunciation of "tu" in the following words from this unit.

eventually  fortune  future opportunity  stupid

Now try pronouncing the following words.

actual  intuition  studio  tulip  tuna

🔲 Listen to the recording to check.

# 4 *Body*

## Cultural Bodies

1 Which of these is not a traditional name for an English pub?
   a) The King's Arms
   b) The Queen's Head
   c) The Prince's Ears

2 What can have two arms and four feet?
   a) a chair
   b) a camera
   c) a dinosaur

3 Which of these superheroes has X-ray vision?
   a) Wonder Woman
   b) Batman
   c) Superman

4 Which band did Rod Stewart use to sing with?
   a) The Faces
   b) The Mouths
   c) The Noses

5 Who starred in *Edward Scissorhands*?
   a) Johnny Depp
   b) Keanu Reeves
   c) Brad Pitt

6 Which of the following is a story by Joseph Conrad?
   a) *Eyes of Happiness*
   b) *Heart of Darkness*
   c) *Mouth of Loch Ness*

## Grammar

**1** Match the advice (a–f) to the pictures (1 and 2).

   a) Dump him.
   b) I really understand how you feel, but maybe you could think it over a little more.
   c) Have you thought of talking it over with your family?
   d) If I were you, I would give some thought to talking it over a little more.
   e) Just tell him to get lost.
   f) You'd be crazy even to think about seeing him again.

**2** Complete the text with phrases from the box.

| | |
|---|---|
| one more thing | if you ask me |
| you could try | why don't you |
| have you tried | if I were you |

a) _____ going to one of those group therapy programs? (b) _____ _____ , they really work. I've been going to one for ages. c) _____ _____ coming along with me next week. (d) _____ come by my place on the way home from work, and we can go together? Then we can both get it off our chests together. Oh, and, (e) _____ , I'd wear something a little more comfortable. And (f) _____ —don't forget your mood ring!

**3** Insert a pronoun (*me/her/him/it*) into each of five sentences below. The other five sentences are correct, and you should not change them.

a) His car broke down on the way to the airport.

b) I took out for dinner on our first, and probably last, date.

c) It finally dawned on that she was seeing another man.

d) The series of robberies is a serious matter, and the police are looking into right now.

e) She said I had really let down by losing my job.

f) The lines were busy, but we managed to get through eventually.

g) The operator asked me to hold on for a few minutes.

h) The plane took off over an hour late.

i) They came to see off at the airport.

j) When you didn't show up last night, we thought you were sick.

**4** Insert a particle from the box into each of five sentences below. The other five sentences are correct, and you should not change them.

| in   on   on   out   up |
| --- |

a) Her request for a divorce came as a complete surprise.

b) How did your driving test go yesterday?

c) How long will it take for you to get ready?

d) If you don't step it, we'll never make it in time.

e) I'll pick you after work and take you to the train station.

f) She always said that she would put her family before her business.

g) The doctors didn't find about his illness until it was too late.

h) This watch hasn't worked in ages.

i) We were completely taken by his lies.

j) You know you can always count me.

**5** Rewrite the sentences, using the words in parentheses. You will need to change the form of some of the verbs.

a) It was a rough night, but you'll recover from it soon.
(get over)
_____
_____

b) You've never disappointed us before!
(let down)
_____
_____

c) What do you think affected him that way?
(come over)
_____
_____

d) It's about time you stopped doing that.
(give up)
_____
_____

e) It was getting late, so I told him to hurry up.
(step on)
_____
_____

f) What kind of a relationship do you have with your parents?
(get along)
_____
_____

g) His story was ridiculous, and we could see immediately that it wasn't true.
(see through)
_____
_____

h) It was her obsession with dieting that finally caused him to leave her.
(drive away)
_____
_____

i) Please leave a message, and I will return your call later.
(call back)
_____
_____

j) I suddenly realized that she wasn't being serious.
(dawn on)
_____
_____

# Listening and Reading

**1** 🔊 Listen to six people talking about a problem, or read the tapescript opposite. Which speaker is someone ...

a) who is a "shopaholic"? ☐

b) who is lonely in a new town? ☐

c) who is overworked and run-down? ☐

d) who keeps forgetting things? ☐

e) whose husband is acting strangely? ☐

f) whose new assistant is not punctual? ☐

**2** 🔊 Listen or read again and answer these questions. Which speaker(s) ...

a) doesn't want to use the telephone? ☐

b) finds it hard to concentrate? ☐

c) likes his/her job a lot? ☐

d) made someone else angry? ☐

e) thought things were better before? ☐

f) have a problem at work? ☐ ☐

**3** Look at the tapescript and find expressions to replace the words in italics.

a) It can't *continue* like this.

b) When she does *begin to do* it, she's fine.

c) It was my turn to *go for* the kids at school.

d) I had to call the police to *force their way into* the house.

e) My mind keeps *wandering*.

f) I don't know *why he is behaving strangely*.

g) He's decided to *begin doing* karate.

**4** 🔊 Now listen to six people responding to the first six speakers. (If you don't have the recording, read the tapescript on p. 79.) Match the second speakers (a–f) to the first speakers (1–6).

a) ☐  b) ☐  c) ☐  d) ☐  e) ☐  f) ☐

Put a check (✔) if the speaker is sympathetic.
Put an X (✘) if the speaker is not sympathetic.

**5** 🔊 Listen again and complete the expressions.

a) I wouldn't _____ with it.

b) Stick your _____ out and make some calls.

c) It's just not _____ anymore.

d) You don't know if you're _____ or _____ .

e) They want things handed to them on a _____ .

**Speaker 1** Well, it's all right, I guess. The job's O.K. and the people are really friendly, but it's when I go home at night. My apartment is nice and everything, but I just sit there and don't know what to do with myself. I write or watch TV, but I really miss going out. I mean, I've only just met my new co-workers, and I don't feel like I can just call them up.

**Speaker 2** I'll have to do something about it. It can't go on like this. Every morning this week—at least twenty minutes, and then she seems to spend the next half hour in the rest room. How long does it take to do your makeup? When she gets into it, she's fine, but the problem is she's just not there enough.

**Speaker 3** Every day, if it's not one thing, it's another. Today it was my keys, yesterday I left the tap running, and one day last week I even forgot to pick the kids up from school. The principal was furious with me. And the children weren't exactly pleased, either. This afternoon, I had to call the police to break into the house. When Derek came home, he hit the roof!

**Speaker 4** I just feel so drained all the time. I have these spots on my chin that won't go away, and it's been really hard to drag myself out of bed in the morning. Then my mind keeps drifting off, and the boss wasn't happy with that report I prepared. I tried to tell him that we'd never meet the deadline, but he doesn't want to hear it. And the migraine I had yesterday!

**Speaker 5** I just don't know what's gotten into him. First it was that yellow and purple Hawaiian shirt; now he's decided to take up karate. I think I liked him better when he just spent all his time pigging out in front of the TV. Now, I look at him and I think, "Who is this guy?"

**Speaker 6** I'd love to come, but I'm pretty low on cash right now. I bought this cool new top at Zara yesterday—it was thirty percent off—and then I saw these Armani jeans on sale. I thought they'd go really well with the purple boots I got last week. Have you seen the new stuff in the Kenzo window? There's a dress that would be perfect for Patsy's wedding. Anyway, as I said, I'm really broke right now.

# Vocabulary

**1** Which word doesn't belong in each of the following groups of words?

a) ankle   knee   lung   heel

b) blood   endorphins   hormones   exercise

c) carbohydrates   fiber   protein   stamina

d) horrible   awful   fabulous   terrible

e) addiction   habit   hooked   lotion

f) advice   obsession   recommendation   tip

g) jogging   rowing   struggling   surfing

h) abandon   chase   give up   quit

**2** Match the beginnings of sentences in box A with their endings in box B.

A

```
a)   After the party, we were left to
b)   Eat some fruit if you have the urge to
c)   He has nobody to
d)   I don't believe her claim to
e)   I'm afraid that a doctor is not available to
f)   It is said that girls are likely to
g)   We were extremely relieved to
h)   You'll always have my shoulder to
```

B

```
1   blame for the trouble but himself.
2   clean up the mess.
3   cry on.
4   mature more quickly than boys.
5   have special healing energy.
6   hear that there was nothing seriously
     wrong.
7   light up a cigarette.
8   see you right now.
```

**3** Complete each sentence with a part of the body from the box.

```
hands   tongue   nose   head
eye   foot   brain   leg
```

a) Don't even try to understand her; she's completely out of her _____ .

b) Ever since she was promoted, she has really looked down her _____ at everyone else.

c) Forget about it; he was just pulling your _____ .

d) I don't think we should trust him; there's more to him than meets the _____ .

e) I meant to say "right," not "left"; it was just a slip of the _____ .

f) She has horses on the _____ ; you can't talk to her about anything else.

g) Taxi drivers know the city like the back of their _____ .

h) The company will _____ the bill.

**4** Now match the idioms in exercise 3 to the definitions below.

*Example*
think you are more important than other people
*look down your nose at other people*

a) crazy

b) know something extremely well

c) tell someone something that isn't true, as a joke

d) pay for something

e) say the wrong thing by accident

f) something/someone is more complicated than you first thought

g) think all the time about one thing

**5** Complete each sentence with a word from the box.

```
available   desperate   effective   essential
reckless   reliable   relieved   flexible
```

a) After a year without a job, she was _____ to find a way to make some money.

b) My father is absolutely _____ in the car and drives like a maniac.

c) She keeps her body _____ by doing a lot of yoga.

d) The medicine will be _____ only if you take it for a week.

e) My car is very _____ ; I haven't had a problem with it yet.

f) We were _____ to get home after that nightmare flight.

g) I'm sorry, nobody is _____ to take your call right now.

h) You're sick because you're not getting enough _____ vitamins and minerals.

**6** Look at the dictionary excerpts and circle the best phrasal verb form in each sentence below.

> **end up**
> **1** If people or things **end up** somewhere, they eventually arrive there, usually by accident. *The result was that the car ended up at the bottom of the canal. The criminal fled with her children, moving from neighborhood to neighborhood and ending up in a friend's basement.*
>
> PHRASAL VERB
> = finish up
> VP prep/adv

> **get by.** If you can **get by** with the few resources you have, you can manage to live or do things satisfactorily. *I'm a survivor, I'll get by. Melville managed to get by on a small amount of money.*
>
> PHRASAL VERB
> = survive
> VP
> VP *on* n

> **settle down**
> **1** When someone **settles down**, he/she starts living a quiet life in one place, especially by getting married or buying a house. *One day I'll want to settle down and have a family. Before she settled down in Iowa, she had her own antique store in San Francisco.*
>
> PHRASAL VERB
> VP
> VP prep/adv

> **put up with**
> **3** If you **put up with** something, you allow it to happen or continue. *It's outrageous, and we won't put up with it anymore.*
>
> PHRASAL VERB
> with neg
> VPP n

> **work up**
> **1** If you **work** yourself **up**, you make yourself feel very upset or angry about something. *She worked herself up into a real state.*
>
> PHRASAL VERB
> V pron-refl P
> into/to n
> V pron-refl P

> **cut down**
> **1** If you **cut down** on something, you consume or do less of it. *He cut down on coffee and cigarettes and ate a balanced diet. If you spend more than your income, can you try to cut down?*
>
> PHRASAL VERB
> VP *on* n

> **get over**
> **1** If you **get over** an unpleasant or unhappy experience or an illness, you recover from it. *It took me a very long time to get over the shock of her death.*
>
> PHRASAL VERB
> VP n

a) If you're not careful, you'll *end up / end you up / end yourself up* where you started—with nothing.

b) With six kids and no husband, it's a wonder she *gets by / gets her by / gets it by*.

c) After three years of traveling, they decided *to settle down / settle it down / settle them down* and start a family.

d) We had to change our approach when she made it clear that she wouldn't *put with it / put up with it / put it up with* any longer.

e) There's no need to *work up you / work you up / work yourself up* about this; it'll all get figured out.

f) You put in too much time at the office, and you really should *cut down it on / cut down on it / cut it down on*.

g) I know it's hard, but you'll *get over / get it over / get over it* soon.

**7** Now write a sentence that is true about you for each of the phrasal verbs in exercise 6.

# Pronunciation

**1** In each of the following groups of words, cross out the word with a different vowel sound.

a) dawn   fault   hot   thought
b) blood   hooked   should   woods
c) call   chance   class   nasty
d) love   jog   lung   tongue

🔲 Listen to the recording to check your answers.

Now decide which group each of the following words should go into, according to the underlined vowel sounds.

> <u>awful</u>   b<u>oo</u>k   t<u>a</u>nned   <u>a</u>nswer
> s<u>u</u>gar   d<u>ou</u>ble   t<u>o</u>ns   l<u>o</u>nger

**2** Decide if the stress should be on the verb or the particle in each sentence.

a) I'll call you back.
b) I don't know what came over me.
c) No, they saw through me.
d) Just put it down, will you?
e) They're going to look into it.
f) You'll soon get over it.
g) I just won't put up with it!

🔲 Listen to check.

**3** 🔲 Listen and repeat after the recording. Each time, the speaker sounds more sympathetic.

a) Oh, no.
b) That's too bad.
c) That must be terrible!
d) How awful for you!

Notice how we make the key word longer when we want to sound more sympathetic.

# Writing

**1** Read the article and choose the best title.

a) The Best TV Programs
b) How to Improve Your Listening
c) Technology Is Best

(1) Their teachers often use their native language to explain the grammar, so it's very strange speaking to another student in a foreign language. In class, there isn't always time to do the listening exercises because it is important to get through the grammar. (2)

Probably the most important thing to remember is that we all need lots of practice. If you haven't already done so, you should definitely consider subscribing to satellite or cable TV channels, such as CNN or BBC World. Even though you might prefer to watch movies, it's important to start with news and current affairs programs that will be closer to your level than the latest thriller. (3)

TV is probably better than radio, but the advantage of radio is that you can do other things at the same time. The BBC World Service and the Voice of America have a good range of programs, and it's a good idea to listen to a wide variety. (4)

Another possibility is to use the Internet. If you have a decent modem, connection, and sound card, there's a huge amount of recorded material that you can download. (5) Maybe, you could encourage friends to start sending you voice mail.

Finally, if you have the opportunity, you definitely ought to consider a trip to an English-speaking country. Washington, Toronto, London, Sydney, Cape Town—it's a huge world, and even a couple of weeks will make an enormous difference. (6) It's not just what you do, but how you feel about it.

**2** Find the place (1–6) in the article where each of the following sentences should go.

a) Again, you don't have to understand everything, but if you're not enjoying it, it's best not to force yourself. ☐

b) All in all, the opportunities are limited. ☐

c) Remember that you need to relax. ☐

d) For many learners of English, one of the biggest problems is improving their listening skills. ☐

e) News, audio/video hookups, and songs (and you can also print out the lyrics) will all help you. ☐

f) Sit back and enjoy what you watch, but don't try to understand everything. ☐

**3** Read the article again and underline any useful expressions for giving advice.

**4** Match each expression in column A with its equivalent in column B.

| A | | B | |
|---|---|---|---|
| a) | alternatively | 1 | actually |
| b) | broadly speaking | 2 | by and large |
| c) | first of all | 3 | in the same way |
| d) | in conclusion | 4 | instead |
| e) | in fact | 5 | naturally |
| f) | in other words | 6 | primarily |
| g) | likewise | 7 | to put it another way |
| h) | moreover | 8 | to start with |
| i) | most of all | 9 | to sum up |
| j) | of course | 10 | what's more |

**5** You are going to write a similar article, titled "How to Improve Your Vocabulary."

In the box, write as many ways of improving your vocabulary as you can think of. These can be ideas that you have already tried or ones that you haven't experimented with yet.

Now decide in which order you will present these ideas. How many paragraphs will you need?

**6** Now write the article. You should write approximately 180 words.

# 5 Ritual

## Ritualized Language

Match the situations to the ritualized language.

| | |
|---|---|
| at a wedding reception | at a funeral |
| at a wedding ceremony | at a political rally |
| on leaving a fast-food restaurant | at the start of a race |
| at the end of a fairy tale | in a court of law |
| before starting a kind of song | |

a) I, Jack Roger Maturin, do solemnly swear to tell the truth, the whole truth, and nothing but the truth.

b) …and they all lived happily ever after.

c) On your marks, get set, go.

d) Ashes to ashes, dust to dust.

e) I would like to propose a toast to the happy couple.

f) Do you, Shane, take this woman, Natasha Tiffany Page, to be your lawful wedded wife?

g) Have a nice day.

h) I woke up this morning with the blues in my head.

i) Ladies and gentlemen, I give you our next governor, Trixie Crooke.

## Grammar

**1** Complete the sentences with words from the box.

> being  dancing  doing(x2)  getting  to do
> to get(x2)  to stand  to rain  to spend  trying

My friend Denise and I didn't want (a) _____ _____ in line all day to get tickets, so she managed (b) _____ some from a friend of her mom's who works at the ticket office. We'd planned (c) _____ the afternoon (d) _____ some shopping at the flea market. But on the weather forecast that morning, they said that they expected it (e) _____ , and we didn't want (f) _____ wet. So we enjoyed ourselves (g) _____ on each other's clothes and (h) _____ our makeup. And Denise taught me (i) _____ the new dance. I could just imagine myself (j) _____ there on the stage with Justin. Anyway, we got there early because I can't stand (k) _____ late. There we were, waiting to get in, when we saw Justin (l) _____ out of his limo! He smiled at me!

**2** Complete each sentence with an -ing form or an infinitive.

a) Please remember _____ (lock) the door on your way out this morning.

b) Do you remember _____ (tell) me that I was the only person in your life?

c) I bet you forgot _____ (bring) the money, didn't you?

d) It was so long ago that I've completely forgotten _____ (say) that. Are you sure?

e) She didn't stop _____ (insult) me all night.

f) They stopped for a minute _____ (get) some money from an ATM on their way to the club.

g) This season, I'm going to try _____ (win) both the 100 and the 200 meters.

h) Try _____ (cook) it in olive oil. It'll taste a lot better.

**3** Complete each sentence with the appropriate form of a verb in the box.

> become  disappoint  do  fail  feel  inform
> teach

a) I can't help _____ that you're not really listening to me.

b) I would hate _____ you, but I don't think I can make it on time.

c) Julia decided to keep on _____ part time until she could find a more interesting job.

d) She went on _____ a triple gold medal winner.

e) Thomas deeply regretted _____ his driving test for the third time.

f) We regret _____ you that your application to the Mathematics Scholar Program has been rejected.

g) When you start _____ the hard part, call me and I'll lend you a hand.

**4** Complete each sentence with a word or phrase from the box.

> constantly   wearing   insisting
> is   keeps   telling   babbling

a) She _____ constantly reading the newspaper.

b) She keeps _____ on watching soap operas.

c) She keeps on _____ about the neighbors all the time.

d) She's _____ writing letters to the editor.

e) She's always _____ saying, "Live and learn."

f) She's always _____ those ugly shoes.

g) I am always _____ her that politicians are all alike.

**5** Change *used to* to *would* whenever it is possible.

Tom Dragoni (a) *used to* be at the top of the FBI's Most Wanted list. Occasionally, he (b) *used to* do jobs for the mob, but he (c) *used to* be best known as America's number one jewel thief. He (d) *used to* live in New York, but the FBI never caught him. As soon as they got close, he (e) *used to* move, sometimes twice a month. He (f) *used to* work most often at some of the exclusive jewelry stores on Fifth Avenue, which he (g) *used to* rob in the middle of the night. He (h) *used to* be so successful because he (i) *used to* never leave any evidence of how he got into the store. But at every store he robbed, he (j) *used to* leave a little card with his name printed on it and the words "Catch me if you can." The police (k) *used to* lie in wait for him week after week, but he was never caught—mostly because he (l) *used to* have so many friends in the FBI itself.

**6** Write nine sentences about the pictures. Three should include *used to*, three *didn't use to*, and three *would*. Use the words in the box to help you.

> be   drink   go   have   like   smoke
> wear   sing   bald   a beard   beer
> a businessman   champagne   cigars
> cigarettes   to clubs   glasses   a hippy
> a cell phone   a ponytail   a suit
> the Rolling Stones

Top: Dave Hanlon, 1973
Bottom: Mr. David M. Hanlon, 2003

*Example*
*He used to sing songs by the Rolling Stones.*

a) _____

_____

b) _____

_____

c) _____

_____

d) _____

_____

e) _____

_____

f) _____

_____

g) _____

_____

h) _____

_____

i) _____

_____

# Reading

**1** Read the short newspaper articles and match the following headlines to the articles.

a) Superstar's Marriage Shocks Fans

b) Couples Cash in by Taking Classes in Marriage

c) My Marriage Is for Life, Insists Hillary

d) Rich Pickings for a Wronged Wife

### 1

**INDIAN film fans were in shock yesterday after discovering that Madhuri Dixit, as popular as Marilyn Monroe ever was in the West, has secretly entered into an arranged marriage.**

Feminists feel Dixit, 32, a fantasy figure for Indian men and star of several blockbusters, has let her more radical sisters down. Few details of her marriage to Shriram Nene, a heart surgeon working in Los Angeles, have emerged, except that it took place in Los Angeles on Oct 17, (**1**). Her two sisters and a brother, who live in the United States, arranged for her to meet Dr. Nene about three months ago. Apparently, the couple's horoscopes matched. According to Rakesh Nath, Dixit's manager, "Madhuri did not fall in love, and so this was the next best way to get married." He added that Dr. Nene "can't speak Hindi, does not watch Hindi movies, and basically doesn't know who he has married."

### 2

HILLARY CLINTON insists that she intends to spend the rest of her life with her husband. She was on the campaign trail for the U.S. Senate when she confronted rumors that she planned to divorce him when he left the White House.

She said, "I certainly intend to spend the rest of my life with him. I have been with my husband for more than half my life. We've been married since 1975, and we have so much between us (2)."

Later, she reaffirmed that she and her husband "love each other very much." When asked why she had discussed such a personal issue, she replied, "Well, I'm not going to anymore." But (3) was seized on by her detractors yesterday as a classic piece of Clintonian equivocation and is unlikely to dampen speculation about the state of their marriage.

### 3

JERRY HALL'S decision to sue for divorce in England has surprised observers because she could have been awarded (4). However, as mother of their four children—Elizabeth, James, Georgia, and Gabriel—she could expect to receive as little as $100 million in England. In addition to the money made through the Rolling Stones, Jagger, (5), has invested in property, cars, antiques, and modern art, among them Andy Warhol originals. He also has an extensive portfolio of stocks and shares.

### 4

IN a move to cut divorce rates in the United States, couples who take classes on marriage before they tie the knot can now receive a discount on a marriage license. The $30 discount scheme, (**6**), is now spreading across the country. It requires couples to attend classes on listening, (**7**), arguing respectfully, and resolving religious and financial differences. States hope that the classes will encourage a more mature approach to marriage and act as a pre-emptive strike against the "negative consequences" of divorce.

**2** Find the places (1–7) in the texts where the following phrases should go.

a) working non-stop since the early 1960s ☐

b) and a lot of love in our family ☐

c) expressing feelings ☐

d) up to half of Jagger's estimated $500 million fortune by an American court. ☐

e) her use of the word "intend" ☐

f) in the presence of a few relatives and friends ☐

g) which was first adopted in Florida ☐

**3** Find words and phrases in the articles that match these definitions.

a) person that many other people dream about (article 1)

b) very successful movies (article 1)

c) the time before an election for a politician (article 2)

d) reduce, limit (article 2)

e) take legal action because you want something (article 3)

f) combination of investments (article 3)

g) reduction in price (article 4)

h) something done to prevent something else from happening (article 4)

**4** Read the stories again and underline the expressions that come before infinitives.

# Vocabulary

**1** Complete each sentence with a word from the box.

| beat | tie | field | game | turnstile |
|------|-----|-------|------|-----------|
| score | victory | win | | |

a) They said they would _____ the championship cup this season, but it didn't happen.

b) It doesn't look as though anyone can _____ her now—she'll get the gold!

c) Angry fans started throwing bottles onto the playing _____ .

d) The coach said that he would not be satisfied with a _____ .

e) The police searched everyone's bag just in front of the _____ .

f) They sang the national anthem at the start of the _____ .

g) His _____ was assured when the other swimmers were disqualified.

h) They'll have to _____ soon if they want to have any chance of getting back into this game.

**2** Find the words below in the word square. The words are written horizontally and vertically, in both directions.

| N | B | R | I | D | E | W | R | B | R |
|---|---|---|---|---|---|---|---|---|---|
| O | M | O | O | R | G | O | I | O | E |
| O | G | U | E | S | T | V | N | U | C |
| M | H | C | E | E | P | S | G | Q | E |
| Y | N | O | M | E | R | E | C | U | P |
| E | K | A | C | A | I | S | L | E | T |
| N | E | C | O | N | F | E | T | T | I |
| O | C | W | I | T | N | E | S | S | O |
| H | I | N | A | M | T | S | E | B | N |
| B | R | I | D | E | S | M | A | I | D |

a) bunch of flowers
b) formal part of a wedding
c) party after a wedding
d) vacation after a wedding
e) jewelry that symbolizes marriage
f) man who accompanies the man getting married
g) man who is getting married
h) formal talk at the wedding reception
i) space for bride's entrance for the ceremony
j) person invited to the wedding

k) person who certifies his/her presence at a wedding by signing a register
l) promise
m) small pieces of paper thrown at a wedding
n) sometimes this is thrown instead of pieces of paper
o) something that is cut at the reception
p) woman who is getting married
q) young girl who accompanies the woman getting married

**3** Match a phrase from box A with a phrase from box B to make a mini-dialogue.

A

| a) | How have you been? |
|----|--------------------|
| b) | I hope you've had a good time. |
| c) | have to be going. |
| d) | Keep in touch. |
| e) | Long time no see. |
| f) | Drive carefully. |
| g) | Thanks. I had a wonderful time. |
| h) | Ted said to say hello. |

B

| 1 | Don't let me keep you. |
|---|------------------------|
| 2 | Not bad, thanks. |
| 3 | Our pleasure. You'll have to come again soon. |
| 4 | O.K. See you. |
| 5 | Thanks. Say hi for me too. |
| 6 | Yes. Thank you for having me. |
| 7 | Yes. What have you been up to lately? |
| 8 | Yes, I'll do that |

**4** Complete each sentence with a word from the box.

| get | give | go | make | set |
|-----|------|----|----|-----|

a) I forgot to _____ the alarm clock last night.

b) We should _____ started if we don't want to be late.

c) I wish I could _____ as much money as she does.

d) Who's going to _____ away the bride at the wedding?

e) Anyone could _____ a mistake like that.

f) Let's _____ through the routine one more time.

→

g) They want to _____ a party for us to meet their friends.

h) His singing is really starting to _____ on my nerves.

i) How much longer is there to _____ ?

j) You forgot to _____ the VCR to record the movie!

k) O.K., I know I was wrong. You don't have to _____ crazy about it.

l) If you want my advice, I'll _____ it to you.

m) Do you think they'll _____ away with it?

**5** Use a dictionary to find the difference between each pair of words.

a) fries/chips

b) behavior/behaviour

c) candy store/sweet-shop

d) crisps/potato chips

e) metre/meter

f) licence/license

g) program/programme

h) symbolise/symbolize

**6** Translate these sentences into your own language.

a) It was nice to see you.

_____

b) Sometimes I translate things.

_____

c) Keep in touch.

_____

d) Nobody but nobody is allowed there.

_____

e) There are a hundred things I'd rather be doing.

_____

Check through the unit again and see if you can find any more useful expressions like these.

_____
_____
_____
_____
_____
_____
_____
_____
_____

# Pronunciation

**1** Decide if the stress is on the first or the second syllable of each of the following words and write the word in the appropriate column.

| alarm | annoy | complain | credit |
| damage | design | indulge | license |
| nonsense | pilot | propose | protect |
| resent | torso | welcome | witness |

Oo                          oO
*title*                     *apart*

_____       _____
_____       _____
_____       _____
_____       _____
_____       _____
_____       _____
_____       _____
_____       _____

Listen to the recording to check your answers.

**2** Listen to the following sentences. Put a check (✔) in the box if the speaker sounds annoyed.

a) He keeps eating too much. ☐

b) He keeps talking with his mouth full. ☐

c) He keeps wiping his nose with his sleeve. ☐

d) He keeps avoiding the housework. ☐

e) He keeps forgetting to polish his shoes. ☐

f) He keeps putting his feet on the sofa. ☐

g) He keeps using cheap aftershave. ☐

h) He can't keep having his way. ☐

Practice using the same intonation as the recording.

# Writing

**1** Put the letter in the correct order.

a) Dear Mr. Gammack,

b) As per our telephone conversation, you are aware that over forty of our guests contracted food poisoning, directly caused by the food you provided.

c) I am writing in reference to the catering services which you provided on October 27 for the wedding reception for my daughter, Benita Molly Shepherd, and her husband.

d) To add insult to injury, I was presented, by one of your staff on my way to the hospital, with a bill which was $20,000 over the agreed price. Under the circumstances, I think my reaction was understandable. I also think that a court of law will find in my favor.

e) Taking all of the above into consideration, I have spoken with an attorney. You will be hearing from him in due time.

f) Your employees, furthermore, were clearly untrained and unsuitable for this kind of work. They provoked a fight when the ambulance arrived, and as a result, my son-in-law, Mr. Vincent Schipani, was arrested.

g) Sincerely,

*Stephen Shepherd*

**2** Find and underline phrases in the letter that mean the same as the following:

a) according to

b) as a direct result of

c) with regard to

d) I was asked to pay

e) above the amount in the contract

f) agree with me

g) when the time is right

h) moreover

i) inappropriate for the job.

**3** Complete each sentence with a phrase from the box.

> a full refund    legal action    apology
> I expect    the matter    your life

a) If I do not hear from you within ten days, I will be obliged to take _____ on this matter.

b) I look forward to receiving _____ _____ as soon as possible.

c) I trust that we will be able to settle _____ _____ amicably.

d) I look forward to receiving a letter of _____ .

e) _____ substantial compensation and a full apology.

You work in the complaint department of a small company. Put the sentences in order of seriousness.

**4** Imagine you are the father of the bride in the story below. The wedding was canceled because of the problems with the rented limo and the driver. Write a letter to the manager of Limo Car Rentals.

# 6 Digital

## Digital Sayings

Match the sayings to the definitions below.

a) He's behind the eight ball.
b) He needs to put two and two together.
c) He was in seventh heaven.
d) He's on it twenty-four seven.
e) He's one up on me.
f) He's back to square one.
g) He has a one-track mind.
h) He's of two minds about it.

1 He can't decide.
2 He's in trouble.
3 He pays constant attention to that.
4 He thinks about only one thing.
5 He should think about it logically.
6 He was really happy.
7 He has an advantage over me.
8 He has to start again.

## Grammar

**1** Write the present participles.

| | | | |
|---|---|---|---|
| admit | _____ | lie | _____ |
| annoy | _____ | occur | _____ |
| assume | _____ | panic | _____ |
| cancel | _____ | settle | _____ |
| chat | _____ | shut | _____ |
| commit | _____ | surf | _____ |
| deliver | _____ | tend | _____ |
| increase | _____ | travel | _____ |

**2** Six of the following sentences are grammatically incorrect. Change the tense to the simple present where necessary.

a) Breakfast is often consisting of no more than a quick cup of coffee.

b) He's recently been devoting five hours a day to his Web site.

c) I don't think that a person's physical appearance is really mattering.

d) Many species of wild animals are becoming rarer.

e) She is really deserving to be congratulated on the wonderful work she has done.

f) She is preferring to spend her time with a good novel.

g) The job is involving a lot of hard work.

h) The number of e-mails we receive is increasing all the time.

i) The price is including the service charge.

**3** Complete each sentence in these pairs with the more appropriate verb form.

*has    is having*

a) She's lucky that she _____ so many friends.

b) He _____ a hard time adjusting to his new home.

*am not seeing    don't see*

c) I _____ anyone later this afternoon. Are you free, too?

d) I _____ myself settling down in the near future.

*do you think    are you thinking*

e) _____ of getting one of those laptops?

f) What _____ of those Internet cafés?

*depends    is depending*

g) He _____ on me to drive him to the airport tomorrow.

h) Do I think you'll pass? Well, it _____ on how hard you have studied.

*are you weighing    do you weigh*

i) How much _____ ?

j) Why _____ that letter? Do you think it needs another stamp?

**4** Complete the sentences with the words in parentheses, using the present perfect.

a) European and American teenagers

_____

to their bedrooms. (always retreat)

b) He _____ to steal from vending machines. (often try)

c) I _____

successful just because of my looks. (not be)

d) I _____
anything stand in my way. (never let)

e) Increasing prosperity _____
_____ to the rise of bedroom
culture. (also contribute)

f) The longest time I _____
_____ on the Net is 24 hours.
(ever spend)

g) This is the hardest crossword puzzle I _____
_____ . (ever do)

**5** Complete the second sentence so that it has a
meaning similar to the first sentence. Use between
two and five words.

a) How long ago did you get your computer?
How long have _____
computer?

b) I've known him since 1995.
I first met _____ 1995.

c) I didn't like him when we met, and I still
don't.
I have _____
from the start.

d) I became a Tomb Raider more than two years
ago.
I've _____
over two years.

e) My trip to Brazil gave me a taste for
adventure.
I have _____
since my trip to Brazil.

f) She began believing in her talent when she
was a child.
She has _____
she was a child.

**6** In five of the sentences below, the present perfect
continuous is used inappropriately. Rewrite each
of those sentences, using an appropriate tense.

a) Bill has been having a few problems with his
computer.

b) Good news! I've just been getting a raise.

c) Have they been arguing?

d) He hasn't been having his birthday party yet.

e) He's been being in a bad car wreck.

f) I've been having enough of your stupid jokes.

g) She's been having some problems at work.

h) She's been having four children, and she's
expecting a fifth.

i) Some of these computer games have been
having a very bad influence on him.

**7** Change each verb in parentheses into the present
perfect or the present perfect continuous.

a) He _____ (cut) the
grass all morning, and he still _____
_____ (not finish).

b) You want to know why it's making that
funny noise? You _____
_____ (drive) with the emergency
brake on!

c) The kids _____
(play) football and will be extremely dirty.

d) We _____ (save) for
a long time, and soon we'll have enough to
buy a new car.

e) A: How long _____
_____ (you/go) out with her?
B: We _____
(know) each other a few weeks.

f) I _____ (look) for a new job
lately, but I _____ _____
(not find) anything interesting yet.

**8** Complete each sentence by using one of the
linking expressions in parentheses.

a) Many parents disapprove of computer games.
_____ they allow their children
to play them because it keeps them quiet.
(Also, As a result, Yet)

b) Computer technology is changing very quickly.
_____ , it is very difficult to know
which computer to buy.
(Consequently, Nevertheless, On the
other hand)

c) More and more people are doing their
shopping on the Internet. _____ ,
the number of Internet companies that fail
remains very high.
(As a result, However, On the other hand)

d) It is predicted that computerized translating
machines will be available very soon.
_____ , people continue to learn
foreign languages.
(Also, Consequently, Nevertheless)

e) Some countries do not teach information
technology in schools. _____ ,
they lack workers with computer skills.
(As a result, Even so, Nevertheless)

# Listening

**1** 🔊 Listen to a radio program about a new kind of Web site. (If you don't have the recording, read the tapescript on p. 79.) Number the pictures in the order in which they are mentioned.

a)

b)

c)

d)

e)

f)

g)

**2** 🔊 Is each of the following sentences true (T) or false (F) according to the reporter on the program?

a) Virtual trips are not as good as real ones. ☐

b) Many people didn't use to have the right software to view WebCams. ☐

c) You can go to camsites only at particular times. ☐

d) NASA took WebCam pictures of the clouds above Mars. ☐

e) The Web site in Birmingham, England, is top-notch entertainment. ☐

f) Hidden WebCams provide some very interesting pictures. ☐

g) The reporter doesn't understand why some people put WebCams in their houses. ☐

h) The reporter often goes swimming in Western Australia. ☐

**3** Look at the tapescript on p. 79 and find words and phrases that mean the same as the following:

a) fashion or trend _____

b) getting onto the Internet _____

c) connected to _____

d) pay money to receive a service _____

e) look at something or visit a place (to find out if it interests you) _____

f) leaving _____

g) 10-9-8-7-6-5-4-3-2-1 _____

**4** Find examples of the present perfect and the present perfect continuous in the tapescript. Match them to the uses of the present perfect in the Language Reference section of your Student's Book.

# Pronunciation

**1** 🔊 Listen to the recording and put these words into three groups, according to the sounds of the underlined letters.

| useful  visible  social  assumed |
|---|
| civilization  delicious  desert  flirtation |
| fussy  losing  mansion  mission |
| oyster  reasonable |

| /s/ | /z/ | /ʃ/ |
|---|---|---|
| useful | visible | social |
| _____ | _____ | _____ |
| _____ | _____ | _____ |
| _____ | _____ | _____ |
| _____ | _____ | _____ |
| _____ | _____ | _____ |

**2** 🔊 Listen to the recording and practice saying the following groups of words.

a) scheme   score   screen   script

b) spacious   special   speed   spreadsheet

c) strange   stuck   strapped   struggle

# Vocabulary

**1** Make compound nouns by combining words from column A with words from column B. Then match the compound nouns to the definitions below.

| A | B |
|---|---|
| Beatles | addict |
| screen | box |
| movie | star |
| juke | media |
| lap | opera |
| milk | shake |
| news | album |
| soap | top |

a) drink containing ice cream

b) TV drama series

c) someone who spends too much time with TV or computer games

d) famous film actor

e) recording of several songs by Paul, John, George, and Ringo

f) machine in an eatery for playing music

g) small portable computer

h) TV, newspapers, Internet, radio

**2** Complete each sentence with an appropriate form of the word in parentheses.

*Example*
I'm sorry—that's my final _____ .
(decide)
I'm sorry—that's my final *decision*.

a) She didn't even notice me. It was as if I had taken an _____ pill. (visible)

b) Customers will appreciate the _____ of the rooms and the speed of the room service. (spacious)

c) He was filled with deep _____ when Lara was cut down by the tomb guard. (sad)

d) It is the _____ of these Pokémon cards that makes them so valuable. (rare)

e) The _____ of the house is broiled lobster in a champagne sauce. (special)

f) Too often, the management neglected the _____ of the workers. (safe)

g) This crossword puzzle's level of _____ is very high. (difficult)

h) You'll find out more about the _____ of this gadget as the game develops. (useful)

**3** Complete each sentence with an appropriate form of a word from the box.

> assume    communicate    contribute
> devote    flirt    install    irritate    navigate

a) The battle of the sexes is often a problem of _____ .

b) The _____ systems were down, and the ship could not locate itself.

c) Susan B. Anthony made important _____ to women's rights.

d) You can imagine my _____ when I found that your e-mail contained a virus.

e) Please wait until the _____ is complete before restarting your computer.

f) She had a brief _____ with her bank manager before realizing it was not a good idea.

g) His idea was based on a false _____ about the economy.

h) Her _____ to her children was absolutely unbelievable.

**4** Complete each sentence with a verb from the box.

> back up    browse    drag    install    paste

a) He was able to _____ his story with hard evidence.

b) I like to _____ around flea markets on the weekend.

c) It was really heavy, so we had to _____ it across the room.

d) The children decided to _____ their pictures onto a huge poster.

e) We're going to _____ a new air-conditioning system in our house.

f) You can click on a file and _____ it to somewhere else on your computer.

g) You can cut a section of text and _____ it somewhere else in the document.

h) You have to _____ a program on your computer before you can use it.

i) You need a program like Internet Explorer if you want to _____ the Net.

j) You should always _____ your computer work on disks just in case you have problems.

# Writing

**1** Read this article about children and computer games and put the paragraphs into the correct order.

1 ☐    2 ☐    3 ☐    4 ☐

**a)**

The first dangers are physical. (1), a child who spends hours in front of a screen is putting his/her eyes under considerable strain. (2), this is time that might otherwise be spent running around and playing outside. The increase in childhood obesity may, at least in part, be attributed to a decrease in healthy physical exercise. There (3) seem to be a number of disadvantages (4) the child's education. We are now experiencing a generation of people who have grown up unaccustomed to doing mental arithmetic or putting pen to paper. (5), the greatest criticism that is leveled at this form of entertainment is moral. What kind of adults will these children become if they think that killing is fun and that guns are toys?

**b)**

It is striking that the criticisms of computer games are usually made by people who are not computer-literate themselves. Games are condemned as immoral or violent, (6) the critics have rarely played them themselves. In fact, many games are highly educational: problem-solving puzzles that encourage both linear and lateral thinking, or strategy games through which we can learn about ancient civilizations or space exploration. What's more, in playing these games, children acquire basic computer skills with file management systems, cursors, and mouse. (7) the violence, it could be argued that there is nothing new here. Children, especially boys, have always played violent games, and they will be fine with a wooden sword or some toy soldiers if deprived of their disk of "Command and Conquer."

**c)**

As with so many things, the answer lies in achieving the right balance. While it cannot be denied that children would be happier and healthier playing Hide and Seek in the yard, for many people, especially the underprivileged, this is simply not possible (no yard!). (8) this, there are worse ways of spending one's time than learning the essential IT skills of modern life.

**d)**

Much has been written about the dangers to young impressionable children of computer games. As parents' lives become busier and as an increasing number of parents seem willing to allow their children to spend hours in front of a computer screen zapping aliens, (9) whether these games are, (10), a harmless pastime or a danger to society and to generations to come.

**2** Find the places (1–10) in the text where the following words or phrases should go.

a) also ☐
b) As for ☐
c) Besides ☐
d) clearly ☐
e) Furthermore ☐
f) However ☐
g) in fact ☐
h) it is time to ask ourselves ☐
i) with regard to ☐
j) yet ☐

**3** You are going to write about whether you prefer to write personal letters or send personal e-mails. Look at the points below and mark each one L for an argument in favor of letters or E for an argument in favor of e-mails.

a) Computers, digital cameras, and Internet accounts are expensive.
b) E-mails encourage meaningless communication.
c) It is cheaper to send e-mails than letters.
d) It is easy to send pictures by e-mail.
e) Letters are friendlier and more personal.
f) Letters are more private than e-mails.
g) Many people prefer to receive letters.
h) People express themselves better and more fully in letters.
i) Sending e-mails is like having a conversation.
j) We spend too much of our time in front of a computer.
k) You can communicate more quickly and more frequently by e-mail.
l) You can write between the lines of the other person's message.
m) You can write to more than one person at the same time.

**4** Now write an article titled "E-mails or Letters: Which Do You Prefer?" Decide which points from exercise 3 you want to include and which you want to omit. Organize your writing into four paragraphs.

1 Introduction: present the topic
2 Points in favor of e-mails
3 Points against e-mails
4 Conclusion/Your opinion

You should write approximately 180 words.

# 7 *Review 1*

## Grammar

**1** Complete the story, using one word in each blank.

A stupid tourist (a) _____ staying in a hotel near a lake (b) _____ was famous (c) _____ its bright blue color. One afternoon, he was sitting on the terrace with a view over (d) _____ lake. When the waiter came (e) _____ take his order, he asked (f) _____ the lake was so blue. The waiter, who was tired of (g) _____ asked (h) _____ the lake all the time, told the man that (i) _____ he came back at the end of the summer, he (j) _____ see the lake being emptied (k) _____ painted blue. To the waiter's surprise, the tourist seemed to accept the explanation. He thought (l) _____ more about him. However, toward (m) _____ end of the summer, the waiter was surprised to see the same tourist. As he took his order, he (n) _____ polite conversation and (o) _____ why the tourist had decided to return. "Well," said the man, "I just (p) _____ to come back and see the painting of the lake bottom."

**2** Each of the following sentences has one word that should not be there. Cross it out.

a) Have you ever been eaten oysters?

b) He's tried to quitting many times.

c) I am always forgetting for to check my e-mail.

d) I don't know how she puts it up with him.

e) If we were having a party, we'd have invite you.

f) If you'd have done your homework, you wouldn't be having these problems.

g) It is sometimes said that a sense of humor is essential for the happiness.

h) It took him a long time to get on over the divorce.

i) It's pretty hard for to get a good job these days.

j) My parents made me to come home by eleven o'clock every night.

k) She was used to swim on the college team.

l) We had lots of the time, so we weren't in a hurry.

**3** Each of the following sentences has one word missing. Insert it.

a) I was wondering you could spare a minute to help me.

b) I've having a hard time lately, and I've had enough.

c) If you had made a mess of your grades in high school, you would have gotten into college.

d) It's extremely important for us find the right person for the job.

e) My boss always insists us arriving by eight thirty.

f) My husband is not interested, and neither I.

g) Our future depends whether we can borrow the money we need.

h) We really don't approve you seeing so much of that man.

i) When gold was discovered in California, Sutter was already one of wealthiest people in the state.

j) You won't forget lock the door when you leave, will you?

**4** Complete each sentence with an appropriate form of the verb in parentheses.

a) After I _____ (play) computer games for about seven hours, my eyes were very tired.

b) He never forgave me for _____ _____ (be) rude to him years ago.

c) He tried _____ (express) his feelings to her, but something always stopped him.

d) I can't stand the way he _____ _____ (always/tell) everyone how good he is.

e) I took aspirin, but it _____ (have) any effect on me yet.

→

f) I would have kept my mouth shut if I
_____ (know) then what I
know now.

g) If I won a lot of money, a yacht is the last
thing I _____ (buy).

h) My hair's wet because I _____
_____ (swim).

i) She smiled at me in a friendly way before she
realized she _____ (forgot)
my name.

j) The conference participants all agreed that the
planet _____ (become)
warmer in the last ten years.

5 Rewrite the second sentence so that it has a
meaning similar to the first sentence, beginning
with the words given.

a) He's always asking embarrassing questions.
He insists _____

_____

b) This is the end of my third year of studying
economics.
I've _____

_____

c) Her lies completely deceived me.
I was completely taken _____

_____

d) If I were you, I wouldn't take it so seriously.
Try not _____

_____

e) What time are they going to arrive?
I'd like to know _____

_____

f) She probably won't object too much.
She is unlikely _____

_____

g) They didn't let us make any noise.
We weren't allowed _____

_____

h) It's because she's so talented that she's been
so successful.
If she weren't _____

_____

6 Fill in each blank by completing the phrasal verb
or adding a preposition.

a) As soon as the children are tucked _____
bed, we can get _____ to our dinner.

b) I get totally fed _____ with the way she
stares _____ me all the time.

c) I really object _____ the way he keeps
_____ talking about his job.

d) I'm beginning to run _____ of patience, so
you'd better not let me _____ this time.

e) If you don't cut _____ on those weight-loss
pills, you'll get addicted _____ them.

f) She tried to take advantage _____ her time
in São Paulo by picking _____ a little
Portuguese.

g) She's really crazy _____ chocolate and
keeps putting _____ weight.

h) The book was made _____ a movie, but it
turned _____ to be a total disaster.

i) You can count _____ him to find a way of
getting away _____ it!

7 Find a response in box B to each conversational
remark in box A.

A

a) Anyway, I'm going to be late. I'd better
be going.
b) Do you mind if I use your phone?
c) Have you tried telling him what you
think?
d) I hardly slept at all. I was so sick.
e) Thanks for having us over. It was nice to
see you again.
f) Paulette said to say hello.
g) What have you been up to lately?
h) What was that all about? I didn't
understand a word of it.

B

1 Give her my best.
2 Don't let me keep you. Give me a call.
3 Neither did I! Not a clue!
4 Nothing much. This and that.
5 Sure, go ahead.
6 Thanks for coming. Drive carefully.
7 No way. He'd kill me!
8 Well, you have only yourself to blame.
You ate too much!

# Vocabulary

**1** Can you find words you have learned in the first half of this book that match the following definitions?

a) the opposite of guilty

I _ _ _ _ _ _ T

b) made to feel small or stupid

H _ _ _ _ _ _ _ _ D

c) strongly advise; try to persuade

U _ _ E

d) businessperson who invests money

E _ _ _ _ _ _ _ _ _ _ R

e) person who earns the most money in a family

B _ _ _ _ _ _ _ _ _ R

f) with no money

B _ _ _ E

g) cure for an illness

R _ _ _ _ Y

h) bunch of flowers

B _ _ _ _ _ T

i) passageway through a plane or theater seats

A _ _ _ E

j) woman on her wedding day

B _ _ _ E

**2** Which word does not belong in each of the following groups of words?

a) casual    neat    notorious    elegant

b) angry    annoyed    irritated    useless

c) afford    aim    intend    plan

d) flood    shovel    stream    trickle

e) carbohydrate    hangover    hay fever    sunburn

f) freak    guy    fan    stuff

g) groom    honeymoon    joke    ring

h) e-mail    laptop    screen    tomb

**3** Complete each sentence with a word from the box.

| food | foot | hands | idea | legs | line |
| lunch | market | neck | pride | | |

a) His latest book certainly gave me a lot of _____ for thought.

b) I don't mind a little inconvenience, but there comes a point when I have to draw the _____ .

c) I really put my _____ in my mouth when I asked about her boyfriend.

d) It's extremely important that this document doesn't fall into the wrong _____ .

e) Our plan is to corner the _____ on online clothes shopping.

f) There really isn't a lot to do in this _____ of the woods.

g) This computer is on its last _____ , and I'll have to get another one.

h) You should know there's no such thing as a free _____ .

i) You'll just have to swallow your _____ and apologize.

**4** Complete each sentence below with a word from the box.

| catch | do | keep | lose |
| make | see | set | take |

a) He _____ fire to his hair while he was lighting a cigarette.

b) He didn't _____ a very good impression on me the first time we met.

c) I've been trying to _____ her eye for ages, but without success.

d) It would be a good idea to _____ a little research before you start the project.

e) She didn't want to _____ contact with her old friends.

f) She works out in a gym twice a day to _____ in shape.

g) We all had a good laugh, but he couldn't _____ the humor in it.

h) You would be foolish to _____ anything he says at face value.

**5** Match a word from column A with a word from column B. Then use these combinations to complete the sentences below.

| A | B |
|---|---|
| balanced | ambition |
| burning | ankle |
| casual | damage |
| cosmetic | diet |
| feature | film |
| half-baked | idea |
| job | look |
| state | prospects |
| twisted | surgery |
| irreparable | championship |

a)  A _____ _____ is probably the most important factor in staying healthy.

b)  A virus on an e-mail attachment can do _____ _____ to your computer.

c)  An MBA would dramatically improve your _____ _____ .

d)  He had some kind of _____ _____ that he could make money by selling secondhand CDs.

e)  Her _____ _____ was always to be a movie star.

f)  I don't think that your medical insurance will pay for _____ _____ .

g)  More and more people are adopting a _____ _____ at work.

h)  What was Antonio Banderas's first _____ _____ ?

i)  She was worried that her leg was broken, but it was only a _____ _____ .

j)  With only three games to go, they're almost certain to win the _____ _____ .

**6** Complete each sentence with an appropriate form of the word in parentheses.

*Example*

It's important to eat a _____ diet.

(balance)

It's important to eat a *balanced* diet.

a)  All you need is a little hard work and _____ . (persevere)

b)  Don't get so _____ ; they'll be here any minute. (patient)

c)  His _____ has been very strange since he had that experience. (behave)

d)  It happened _____ ; nobody is to blame. (accident)

e)  She couldn't hide her _____ with the children. (annoy)

f)  The _____ of oil in the Eastern Plains changed the Colombian economy. (discover)

g)  The company has been running _____ for many years. (profit)

h)  The movie is an _____ of a novel by Edith Wharton. (adapt)

i)  The pool is for the _____ of hotel guests only. (convenient)

j)  They were _____ rude at the party. (embarrass)

**7** Match the beginnings of sentences in box A with their endings in box B.

A

| |
|---|
| a)  He went jogging regularly. Nevertheless, |
| b)  He's hopeless at anything technical, whereas |
| c)  His advice is not worth having. Moreover, |
| d)  I shouldn't have any problem as long as |
| e)  I spent the weekend at Robert's house. Oh, by the way, |
| f)  I'm going to think it over until |
| g)  The factory was closed, and as a result, |
| h)  The groom started eating the cake while |

B

| | |
|---|---|
| 1 | four hundred people lost their jobs. |
| 2 | he asked me to say hello for him. |
| 3 | he was unable to lose weight. |
| 4 | he will charge you for his time. |
| 5 | his wife is a real expert. |
| 6 | I remember to set the alarm clock. |
| 7 | the best man was making his speech. |
| 8 | I'm sure of what I'm doing. |

# Tapescripts

(reference page 78)

## 1 Images

**Host** ...and on this week's *Stars from the Past*, we ask you to name four megastars, known as much for the way they look as for the way they sing. First prize is two tickets to this year's MTV awards, so get your pens ready and give us a call. Lines are open now. Number one.

**Voice 1** Starting life as a pianist in a suburban London bar, fat Reg Dwight, as he was then known, has come a long way. His first experiments with fashion were with a variety of outrageous hats to hide the fact that he was bald. Poor guy, his eyesight wasn't much good either, and his taste in trashy plastic glasses was S-A-D spells *sad*. Now firmly middle-aged, for his fiftieth birthday he dressed as a cross between Louis the Sixteenth and Marie Antoinette, with a huge platinum-blond curly wig, rouge, eyeliner, and a beauty spot. His outfits got worse, and so did his music. But bald and putting on weight, he had to do something...

**Host** Got it? Prick up your ears for number two.

**Voice 2** Kicking off his life of fame as a cute little kid with an outsize Afro curl, this one changed fast. In fact, he changed so much, he even seemed to change color. To everyone's surprise, he did get married, but he always preferred the company of monkeys and children. His music was a clever pastiche of different styles, and, man, could he dance! His video clips were legendary, and he is probably best remembered as a zombie. But was he cool? Was he cool? He sure was, if you were ten years old at the time.

**Host** This is X-CON FM, and I'm Dezz the Big O. Next on the block, number three.

**Voice 1** A prima donna with an innocent face, and another star for your younger sister. This one is said to have demanded pink toilet paper in every hotel. But back to the point. Can anyone remember her music? Didn't one of them go dum-de-dum-de-da or something? Anyway, who cares?

**Host** Yes...one of my favorites, too. Ready for number four?

**Voice 2** Now, this one was really cool. Back in the 1980s, he seemed to prefer bikinis and raincoats, but he had a large wardrobe of tight corsets and shiny tights, and who knows what else. At the age of 25, he announced that he was going to retire, to look "for the ladder."

What was he talking about? Don't even try to understand. This is a star who changed his name to a symbol that can't even be pronounced...we're talking seriously strange.

**Host** O.K., enough of that. Back to business.

## 3 Money

**Voice-over** Wheel of Chance. With Danny McDee. Put your hands together for your host with the most. (applause)

**Danny** They say that money makes the world go around, but on this show it's the wheel that makes the money go around! Come take a spin with the wheel of chance and see how many of my prizes you can take home.

**Voice-over** And what a choice of goodies we have tonight—with a jackpot of ten thousand dollars.

**Danny** Come play and take a spin. Who's up for it tonight?

**Voice-over** Margaret Short is from Chicago, and she works in the fast-food industry. Can she be fast enough tonight? Germaine Becket is from Toronto and works in a bakery. Will she be today's breadwinner? And Claire Borges is a bank teller from Los Angeles. How profitable will her evening be? Well, there you go. Margaret, Germaine, Claire—you're on!

**Danny** Are you ready to start? There's a lot at stake. Who's going to take home tonight's jackpot? The first game is on the board, with tonight's mystery phrase, which has seven words.

O.K., contestants—let's get things rolling! Now, the first one to answer this question correctly will start the game. Fingers on the buzzer. Where is the Grand Canyon? (*buzzer*)

**Margaret** Is it in California?

**Danny** Nice try, but... (*buzzer*)

**Claire** Is it in Arizona?

**Danny** Yes, it is in Arizona. (*applause*) Spin the wheel. (*spinning noise*) Fifty dollars. Fifty dollars if you guess a letter from tonight's mystery phrase.

**Claire** Can I have a "D" as in "doughnut," please?

**Danny** No, sorry. Too bad—but don't worry, Claire. Margaret, your turn... (*spinning noise*) A hundred dollars—if you guess one of those letters!

**Margaret** Can I have an "F" as in "fries," please? (*negative beep*)

**Danny** Oh, too bad. Germaine. (*spinning noise*) Two hundred dollars!

**Germaine** "M" as in "money," please. (*two positive beeps*)

**Danny** Yes, there are two of them. That's two times two hundred—four hundred dollars! You're in control, Germaine. Take another shot at it. (*spinning noise*) One hundred dollars!

**Germaine** I'll have an "O" as in "orange," please. (*four positive beeps*)

**Danny** And another four! That's another four hundred bucks. Hit that wheel! (*spinning noise*) Ooooh, miss a turn. Too bad! And you were doing so well. Claire. (*spinning noise*) Five hundred dollars!!!

**Claire** "L" as in "love," please, Danny. (*negative beep*)

**Danny** Nope, nothing doing, Claire. It's not your day, is it? Margaret. (*spinning noise*) One hundred dollars.

**Margaret** "M" as in "mother," please.

**Danny** We've already had "M." Try again.

**Margaret** "Y" as in "yellow," please, Danny. (*three positive beeps*)

**Danny** You really struck gold here. You just won three times one hundred dollars. Spin that wheel again. (*spinning noise*) Five hundred dollars! But will you get another of those letters?

**Margaret** "T" as in...oh, let's see— "two." (*two positive beeps*)

**Danny** You just won one thousand dollars! Can you guess the secret phrase, Margaret? Cross your fingers.

**Margaret** Is it "Your money or your life"?

**Danny** That doesn't fit. Too bad.

**Margaret** I know. It was just a wild guess.

**Danny** Germaine, you miss this turn, so, Claire, over to you. (*spinning noise*)

**Danny** Fifty dollars.

**Claire** "R" as in "romance," please, Danny. (*three positive beeps*)

**Danny** Yes! There are three of them, so that's a hundred and fifty dollars to you.

**Claire** Can I guess the phrase, please, Danny?

**Danny** Go for it! Good luck!

**Claire** Is it "Put your money where your mouth is"?

**Danny** We have a winner! Claire Borges from Los Angeles wins five thousand dollars! And that's on top of the one hundred fifty dollars she already had. Now Claire, come with me behind the curtain and get ready for the jackpot challenge.

(reference page 79)

## 4 Body

a) "You'd better keep an eye on him. There's something funny going on. I wouldn't put up with it if I were you. You don't know where you stand with a man like that. You poor thing! Sounds like my Derek before he went off the deep end. I don't know why you never settled down with that guy Dave you used to date. At least you knew where you stood with him."

b) "Oh, wow! You look like death warmed over. You can't let it get to you like that. Why don't you just take a few days off. Say you're stressed out and need some time off. That's what I would do."

c) "I don't know what you're getting so worked up about. You've been there only a couple of weeks. Just stick your neck out and make a few phone calls, for goodness sake! You can't expect people to just come knocking on your door. You'll get by—just be patient."

d) "Oh, don't give me that. It's always the same. Don't you have enough stuff? Most of it ends up in the garbage anyway before you announce, 'It's just not me anymore!' And if I tell you tomorrow that we had a great time, don't start feeling sorry for yourself. You have nobody to blame but yourself."

e) "I know. It's awful when that happens. One minute everything's going along smoothly, and the next minute you don't know whether you're coming or going. My son says it's my age, but what does he know? I'm sure your children weren't that upset, were they? Happens to me all the time."

f) "I know exactly what you mean. I don't know why some of them even bother. They seem to expect things to be handed to them on a silver platter. Have you tried calling the agency to see if they can send you another one? And if that's the best they can do, have you thought of trying another agency?"

## 6 Digital

**Host** We'll be returning to your list of top Web sites later in the program, but first a look at a new craze that is sweeping the Net. If you didn't manage to make travel arrangements last week with lastminute.com, probably the next best thing is a virtual trip on the Net. We're talking here about the wonderful world of WebCams. Our webmaster, Christine Bolton, has been logging on and finding the best places to go. Christine.

**Christine** Well, there's really nothing especially new about WebCams, but it's only recently that large numbers of people have had the software on their computers that allows them to access a cam. Essentially, a WebCam is just a digital camera hooked up to an Internet connection, allowing surfers to watch whatever the camera is pointing at in real time. What we're seeing more and more these days is concerts broadcast to Internet viewers who subscribe to music sites.

**Host** What's the difference between a WebCam and a TV?

**Christine** The end result is pretty much the same, although the technology is very different. The big difference is the potential of the Net, but now that digital TV has arrived, things are changing fast. With TV, you still have to wait until the time that what you want to watch is actually on, but with the Net, you can go to a camsite anytime you want.

Things really got going back in 1997, when NASA attached cameras to the robot vehicle that was exploring the surface of the planet Mars. The cameras were hooked up to a Web site, and you could watch these pictures on your screen live and direct. The quality of the pictures has improved a lot since then. Right now there's a similar robot buggy exploring parts of the Andes in South America, and you can follow its progress in the mountains above the clouds.

**Host** That sounds incredible! Are there any camsites that you would particularly recommend?

**Christine** Well, to be honest, most of them are pretty boring. Many cities have WebCams set up in various places. New York has some interesting ones where you can look at famous sights, like the Statue of Liberty, from strange angles. But many are just plain boring. There's one of a street in Birmingham, England, and all you can see is the sidewalk, and every now and then you see a shoe walk by. It's not exactly top-notch entertainment. And there are others that show traffic—but you'd have to be seriously sad to want to spend much time watching that.

**Host** What else is good for the virtual tourist?

**Christine** Well, you can get some very pretty pictures from one that covers Mount Fuji in Japan, and there's another in—hang on, I'll try to pronounce this right—in Popocatepetl in Mexico. It's an amazing volcano with smoke coming out of it and everything. It's awesome.

**Host** You hear a lot about secret cams. What's the story behind them?

**Christine** It's true there are a small number of secret cams, hidden in public restrooms and places like that, but even the traffic is interesting compared to this. There are also some sad freaks who set up WebCams in their houses, so that you can watch them brushing their teeth or sleeping. Don't ask why!

**Host** What's your personal favorite?

**Christine** The best I've found is a wonderful site where you can look at a beach in Western Australia. The site was set up for surfers—real surfers, that is—who want to check out the waves before heading for the beach. But I love it—I've been there twice already this morning. I find it so relaxing—and there are quite a few beaches to choose from.

**Host** Thanks, Christine. For details of all these WebCams, check out our own Web site: www.radiozine.org. Now back to our countdown of the sites you voted for…

**42**   *Split Edition Book A* | Units 1–7   *Tapescripts*

# Answer key

## 1 Images

### Images, Pictures, and Paintings

**1**  a) image  b) image  c) painting  d) picture
    e) picture  f) painting

**2**  a) 2  b) 6  c) 1  d) 3  e) 5  f) 4

### Grammar

**1**  a) just bought  b) was walking  c) saw
    d) had been looking  e) just had  f) am going
    g) goes  h) will be  i) is wearing

**2**  b) Does anyone in your family ~~does~~ speak English
       fluently?
    e) Is there anybody in your family who ~~does~~ wears a fur
       coat?
    g) When was the last time you ~~have~~ read your horoscope?
    h) Who were you ~~were~~ speaking to last night?

**3**  a) Do you realize I *have* gotten tired of telling you?
    e) Where were you when you *were* needed?
    f) Who did you say you *were* going out with?
    h) Why *did* you not tell me you were married?

**4**  a) So does  b) So is  c) Neither has  d) So did
    e) So does/has  f) Neither has  g) Neither was
    h) So was
    Sentence pairs c), f), and h) are completely untrue.

**5**  a) do/have they  b) did she  c) aren't I
    d) haven't you  e) don't they  f) does she
    g) do they  h) shall we

**6**  a)  I'd like to know what your biggest secret is.
    b)  I was wondering when you had your first kiss.
    c)  I want to know if/whether you are going out with
       anyone.
    d)  I was wondering who the last person you talked to
       was.
    e)  I'd like to know who/whom you dislike the most.
    f)  Could you tell me if/whether you have ever broken
       the law?
    g)  I want to know if you take vitamins.
    h)  Do you think you could answer these questions
       truthfully?

### Listening

**1**  a)  Michael Jackson      excerpt 2
    b)  Mariah Carey        excerpt 3
    c)  Prince              excerpt 4
    d)  Elton John          excerpt 1

**2**  a) P  b) EJ  c) MJ  d) EJ  e) P  f) MJ  g) MC
    h) EJ and P  i) MJ and MC

**3**  a) 4  b) 8  c) 5  d) 7  e) 1  f) 2  g) 6  h) 3

**4**  a) for  b) as  c) in  d) on  e) to  f) of  g) at
    h) to  i) of  j) to  k) of

### Pronunciation

a) A  b) B  c) A  d) A  e) A  f) B

### Vocabulary

**1**  a) resemblance  b) talent  c) eye  d) platinum
    e) image  f) detail  g) ambition  h) time
    i) thing

**2**  a) go  b) go  c) take  d) affect  e) put  f) look
    g) do  h) have  i) lose  j) make  k) swallow

**3**  a) 7  b) 1  c) 4  d) 2  e) 5  f) 6  g) 3

**4**

| | | |
|---|---|---|
| adaptable | adaptation | adapt |
| ambitious | ambition | – |
| – | emergence | emerge |
| impressive | impression | impress |
| innocent | innocence | – |
| strategic | strategy | – |
| tempting | temptation | tempt |

**5**  a) tempt  b) emerge  c) strategic  d) ambition
    e) innocence  f) tempt  g) adapt

### Writing

**1**  c) The cost of an image

**2**  *Suggested answers*
    i    The things we buy
    ii   The trade in counterfeit goods
    iii  Where the money goes
    iv  Think again

**3**  If you walk down any street in any town anywhere, you'll
    see them. The Levi's jeans, a Tommy Hilfiger T-shirt, Nike
    sneakers and, perhaps, a pair of Ray-Bans. Oh, don't forget
    the Rolex watch and possibly a scent of what might just be
    a Calvin Klein perfume. It could be you, and it could be
    me. Almost all of us, at some point in our lives, buy
    something because of the name that is printed on it. We
    buy an image, and we are prepared to pay for it.

    But how many of these products are the real thing? None
    of the big companies will admit how much they lose, but
    the counterfeit trade runs into billions of dollars each year.
    On London's Oxford Street or the streets of New York, it's
    easy to buy fake labels for a fraction of the normal price.

    If you're really low on cash, there's an even better way of
    doing it. If you know the right person, you can buy a bag
    of fake Lacoste crocodiles. Sew these onto some cheap
    T-shirts. Keep a few for yourself and sell the rest to your
    friends.

    Does anybody care? Not many of us are likely to have
    much sympathy for the big fashion companies. Surely they
    can afford it. But stop for a minute and think about where
    all the money goes. The police now have growing evidence
    that much of the money goes back into drug dealing. Some
    terrorist organizations are funded by counterfeit goods and
    supported by profits made from the sale of fake T-shirts.

    So, next time you're tempted by a cheap T-shirt or some
    other knockoff, think again. Make sure you know where
    your money is really going.

**4**  afford  evidence  lives  almost  favorite  million
    sympathy  companies  friends  perfume  terrorist

## 2 Family

### Grammar

**1** a) They couldn't afford to buy me lots of new clothes. / They couldn't afford lots of new clothes for me.
b) They always reminded me to do my homework.
c) They encouraged me to go to church every week.
d) They never let me bring friends home.
e) They made me come home at ten o'clock every night.
f) They warned me not to go to nightclubs. / They warned me about nightclubs and said that I shouldn't go to them.
g) My father expected me to work in his factory.
h) My parents taught me to respect authority. / My parents taught me about respecting authority.
i) They would have liked me to be like them.
j) I managed to run away from home when I was 14.

**2** a) doing   b) to help   c) to do   d) to clean
e) looking   f) being   g) getting   h) coming
i) to come

**3** a) on   b) on   c) of   d) from   e) to   f) to
g) about   h) of   i) on   j) for   k) for

**4** a) hopeless   b) angry   c) proud   d) afraid
e) allergic   f) covered   g) used   h) fond
i) interested   j) essential

**5** a) He didn't want ~~that~~ his friends to find out about his father's job.
b) His father made him ~~to~~ join in the act.
c) I've considered ~~of~~ buying my own apartment, but I can't afford to.
d) We'd want ~~for~~ them to do well in school.
e) I look forward to ~~be~~ hearing from you.
f) Gina's mom manages ~~her~~ to stay in shape.
g) My father taught ~~for~~ me to swim when I was five.
h) We'd warn them ~~about~~ not to take drugs.
i) I never waste time ~~at~~ ironing my clothes.
j) They let her ~~to~~ have what she wants all the time.
k) We can't afford ~~us~~ to stay at an expensive hotel.
l) We ~~are~~ tend to work late.

### Pronunciation

thin, stick, middle
next, head, register
can't, black, happen
knock, father, shopping
off, bought, daughter
look, could
son, flood, hug

### Reading

**1** Photo a)

**2** a) F   b) F   c) F   d) T   e) T   f) F   g) F
h) T   i) F   j) T

**3** a) on   b) at   c) Of   d) with   e) to   f) like
g) in   h) for

**4** a) woes   b) loquacious   c) wound up
d) fugitive   e) wee lad   f) peculiar

### Vocabulary

**1** a) allergic   b) compatible   c) embarrassed/embarrassing
d) fond   e) humiliated/humiliating   f) impatient
g) dependent/dependable

**2** a) allergy   b) dependence   c) fond   d) humiliated
e) embarrassment   f) compatible   g) impatient

**3** a) social class   b) table manners   c) college degree
d) Sunday brunch   e) family background
f) country cottage   g) job prospects

**4** 1 a)   2 g)   3 b)   4 c)   5 d)   6 j)   7 e)   8 h)   9 i)
10 f)   11 k)

### Writing

**1** 1 d)   2 e)   3 m)   4 n)   5 i)   6 k)   7 c)   8 l)   9 f)
10 g)   11 a)   12 j)   13 b)   14 h)

**2** a) P   b) H   c) H   d) H   e) P   f) H   g) P   h) P
i) P   j) H

## 3 Money

### Money Songs

a) Money, money, money, must be funny, in the rich man's world (Abba)
b) I don't care too much for money 'cause money can't buy me love (The Beatles)
c) Money for nothing and chicks for free (Dire Straits)
d) Money, it's a crime; share it fairly but don't take a slice of my pie (Pink Floyd)
e) Money's too tight to mention; I can't even qualify for my pension (Simply Red)

### Grammar

**1**

| with *the* | without *the* |
| --- | --- |
| Atlantic | Argentina |
| Caribbean | China |
| Gulf of Mexico | India |
| Middle East | Lake Superior |
| Gobi Desert | Mecca |
| Andes | Mount Everest |
| moon | Africa |
| Amazon River | Texas |
| European Union | Venus |

**2** a) ~~The~~ credit cards are what ~~the~~ people use after they discover that money can't buy everything. (anon.)
b) ~~The~~ empty pockets make ~~the~~ empty heads. (William Carlos Williams)
c) ~~The~~ life is short, and so is ~~the~~ money. (Bertolt Brecht)
d) ~~The~~ money can't buy ~~the~~ friends, but you can get a better class of enemy. (Spike Milligan)
e) ~~The~~ money is better than ~~the~~ poverty, if only for ~~the~~ financial reasons. (Woody Allen)
f) ~~The~~ money isn't everything. There are also ~~the~~ credit cards and ~~the~~ traveler's checks. (anon.)
g) The poor have more children, but the rich have more relatives. (anon.)

**3** a) A   b) a/the   c) the   d) a   e) a   f) the   g) the
h) the   i) the   j) a   k) the   l) the   m) The   n) the
o) The

**4**  a) the  b) a  c) an  d) –  e) a  f) the  g) a
h) an  i) –  j) –  k) The  l) The  m) an  n) a
o) –  p) a  q) the  r) the  s) –  t) a  u) –
v) a  w) a  x) the

**5**  a)  If you *were* the president of your country, what would you do about the environment?
b)  If I ~~did~~ ever had the chance, I'd take a year off and travel.
c)  If I could live anywhere in the world, I'd probably *buy* a beach villa in Tahiti.
d)  If I didn't need to learn English for my job, I would *have stopped* a long time ago.
e)  If I *hadn't* come to school yesterday, I would have stayed home.
f)  If I *had known* this was going to be so difficult, I would never have started it.
g)  If I *had exercised* more when I was younger, I would be in better shape now.
h)  If I *had been* born with very rich parents, I wouldn't be working at this job, would I?

**6**  a) 4  b) 3  c) 2  d) 8  e) 5  f) 7  g) 6  h) 1

**7**  *Suggested answers*
a)  If I'd known you were broke, I would've offered to pay.
b)  If it were made of real gold, it would be worth a lot.
c)  If they hadn't cornered the market, they wouldn't have raised the price.
d)  If he didn't have a talent for spotting a golden opportunity, he wouldn't have made millions.
e)  If she had realized it was valuable, she wouldn't have given it away.
f)  If my time weren't /wasn't so precious, I would've spoken to them.
g)  If I were you, I'd get a job.

## Listening

**1**  a)  Margaret—Burger Whiz manager—Chicago
b)  Germaine—baker—Toronto
c)  Claire—bank teller—Los Angeles

**2**  D doughnut  F fries  M money  O orange
L love  Y yellow  T two  R romance

**3**

| Margaret | Germaine | Claire |
|---|---|---|
| $300 | $400 | $150 |
| $1000 | $400 | $5000 |
| Total: $1300 | Total: $800 | Total: $5150 |

**4**  Put your money where your mouth is.

**5**  a) hands  b) stake  c) buzzer  d) struck
e) wild

**6**  a) goodies  b) get things rolling
c) take another shot at it  d) bucks  e) nothing doing
f) cross your fingers  g) go for it

## Vocabulary

**1**  1 a)  2 b)  3 b)  4 c)  5 a)  6 c)  7 a)  8 b)

**2**  a) give  b) made  c) taken  d) caused  e) take
f) make  g) have  h) make  i) set  j) cause  k) make

**3**  a) flood  b) drifting  c) food  d) mull  e) baked
f) stream  g) digest

**4**  a) handful  b) happiness  c) significance
d) persecution  e) wisdom  f) capitalize
g) profitably  h) appointment  i) arrival
j) valuable

## Writing

**1**  a) By the time  b) as  c) As soon as / When
d) until  e) When  f) As  g) as/while
h) During  i) Just as / When  j) Then

## Pronunciation

**3**  a) a few weeks
b) as soon as they come
c) food for thought
d) it won't matter to me
e) make a mess of things
f) the click of a camera

---

# 4  Body

## Cultural Bodies

1 c)  2 a)  3 c)  4 a)  5 a)  6 b)

## Grammar

**1**  1 a) e) f)
2 b) c) d)

**2**  a) Have you tried  b) If you ask me
c) You could try  d) Why don't you
e) if I were you  f) one more thing

**3**  b)  I took *her/him* out for dinner on our first, and probably last, date.
c)  It finally dawned on *her/me* that she was seeing another man.
d)  The series of robberies is a serious matter, and the police are looking into *it* right now.
e)  She said I had really let *her/him* down by losing my job.
i)  They came to see *her/him/me* off at the airport.

**4**  d)  If you don't step *on* it, we'll never make it in time.
e)  I'll pick you *up* after work and take you to the train station.
g)  The doctors didn't find *out* about his illness until it was too late.
i)  We were completely taken *in* by his lies.
j)  You know you can always count *on* me.

**5**  a)  It was a rough night, but you'll get over it soon.
b)  You've never let us down before!
c)  What do you think came over him?
d)  It's about time you gave that up/gave up doing that.
e)  It was getting late, so I told him to step on it.
f)  How do you get along with your parents?
g)  His story was ridiculous, and we could see through it immediately.
h)  It was her obsession with dieting that finally drove him away.
i)  Please leave a message, and I will call (you) back later.
j)  It suddenly dawned on me that she wasn't being serious.

## Listening and Reading

**1**  a) 6  b) 1  c) 4  d) 3  e) 5  f) 2

**2**  a) 1  b) 4  c) 1  d) 3  e) 5  f) 2, 4

**3**  a) go on  b) get into  c) pick (the kids) up
d) break into  e) drifting off
f) what's gotten into him  g) take up

**4** a) 5 [✔]  b) 4 [✔]  c) 1 [✘]  d) 6 [✘]
   e) 3 [✔]  f) 2 [✔]

**5** a) stand  b) neck  c) me  d) coming, going
   e) silver platter

## Vocabulary

**1** a) lung  b) exercise  c) stamina  d) fabulous
   e) lotion  f) obsession  g) struggling  h) chase

**2** a) 2  b) 7  c) 1  d) 5  e) 8  f) 4  g) 6  h) 3

**3** a) head  b) nose  c) leg  d) eye  e) tongue
   f) brain  g) hands  h) foot

**4** a) out of your head
   b) know something like the back of your hand
   c) pull someone's leg
   d) foot the bill
   e) make a slip of the tongue
   f) there's more to it/him/her than meets the eye
   g) have something on the brain

**5** a) desperate  b) reckless  c) flexible  d) effective
   e) reliable  f) relieved  g) available  h) essential

**6** a) end up  b) gets by  c) settle down
   d) put up with it  e) work yourself up
   f) cut down on it  g) get over it

## Pronunciation

**1** a) hot  b) blood  c) call  d) jog
   Group a) awful, longer
   Group b) tanned, answer
   Group c) carbon, karate
   Group d) double, tons

**2** The particle is stressed in each sentence; the first particle is stressed in g).

## Writing

**1** b)

**2** a) 4  b) 2  c) 6  d) 1  e) 5  f) 3

**4** a) 4  b) 2  c) 8  d) 9  e) 1  f) 7  g) 3  h) 10
   i) 6  j) 5

# 5 Ritual

## Ritualized Language

a) in a court of law
b) at the end of a fairy tale
c) at the start of a race
d) at a funeral
e) at a wedding reception
f) at a wedding ceremony
g) on leaving a fast-food restaurant
h) before starting a kind of song (a blues song)
i) at a political rally

## Grammar

**1** a) to stand  b) to get  c) to spend  d) doing
   e) to rain  f) to get  g) trying  h) doing
   i) to do  j) dancing  k) being  l) getting

**2** a) to lock  b) telling  c) to bring  d) saying
   e) insulting  f) to get  g) to win  h) cooking

**3** a) feeling  b) to disappoint  c) teaching  d) to become
   e) failing  f) to inform  g) to do

**4** a) is  b) insisting  c) babbling  d) constantly
   e) keeps  f) wearing  g) telling

**5** These can be changed to *would*: b), e), f), g), i), j), k).

**6** *Possible answers*
   He used to be a hippy/drink beer/have a beard/ have a
   pony-tail/like the Rolling Stones/smoke cigarettes.
   He didn't use to be a businessman/be bald/drink
   champagne/have a cell phone/smoke cigars/wear a tie/
   wear glasses.
   He would drink beer/go to clubs/smoke cigarettes.

## Reading

**1** a) 1  b) 4  c) 2  d) 3

**2** a) 5  b) 2  c) 7  d) 4  e) 3  f) 1  g) 6

**3** a) fantasy figure  b) blockbusters  c) campaign trail
   d) dampen  e) sue  f) portfolio  g) discount
   h) pre-emptive strike

**4** arranged for her, this was the next best way,
   she intends, she planned, is unlikely,
   Jerry Hall's decision, she could expect, in a move,
   it requires couples

## Vocabulary

**1** a) win  b) beat  c) field  d) tie  e) turnstile
   f) game  g) victory  h) score

**2** a) bouquet  b) ceremony  c) reception  d) honeymoon
   e) ring  f) best man  g) groom  h) speech  i) aisle
   j) guest  k) witness  l) vow  m) confetti  n) rice
   o) cake  p) bride  q) bridesmaid

**3** a) 2  b) 6  c) 1  d) 8  e) 7  f) 4  g) 3  h) 5

**4** a) set  b) get  c) make  d) give  e) make  f) go
   g) give  h) get  i) go  j) set  k) go  l) give  m) get

**5** a) fries (US)/chips (UK)
   b) behavior (US)/behaviour (UK)
   c) candy store (US)/sweet-shop (UK)
   d) crisps (UK)/potato chips (US)
   e) metre (UK)/meter (US)
   f) licence (noun in UK)/license (verb in UK, noun and
      verb in US)
   g) program (US)/programme (UK)
   h) symbolise (UK)/symbolize (US)

## Pronunciation

**1**
| Oo *title* | oO *apart* |
| --- | --- |
| credit | alarm |
| damage | annoy |
| licence | complain |
| nonsense | design |
| pilot | indulge |
| torso | propose |
| welcome | protect |
| witness | resent |

**2** b) ✔  c) ✔  f) ✔  g) ✔

## Writing

**1** The correct order is a), c), b), f), d), e), g).

**2**
- a) As per
- b) directly caused by
- c) in reference to
- d) I was presented ... with a bill
- e) over the agreed price
- f) find in my favor
- g) in due time
- h) furthermore
- i) unsuitable for this kind of work

**3** a) legal advice  b) a full refund  c) the matter
d) apology  e) I will expect

most serious  a)  e)  b)  d)  c) least serious

---

# 6 Digital

## Digital Sayings

a) 2  b) 5  c) 6  d) 3  e) 7  f) 8  g) 4  h) 1

## Grammar

**1** admitting, annoying, assuming, canceling, chatting, committing, delivering, increasing, lying, occurring, panicking, settling, shutting, surfing, tending, traveling

**2**
- a) Breakfast often consists of ...
- c) ... physical appearance really matters.
- e) She really deserves to be ...
- f) She prefers to ...
- g) The job involves a lot ...
- i) The price includes the ...

**3** a) has  b) is having  c) am not seeing  d) don't see
e) Are you thinking  f) do you think  g) is depending
h) depends  i) do you weigh  j) are you weighing

**4** a) have always retreated  b) has often tried
c) haven't been  d) have never let
e) has also contributed  f) have ever spent
g) have ever done

**5**
- a) you had your
- b) him in
- c) not liked him / disliked him
- d) been a Tomb Raider (for)
- e) had a taste for adventure
- f) believed in her talent since

**6**
- b) Good news! I've just gotten a raise.
- d) He hasn't had his birthday party yet.
- e) He's been in a bad car wreck.
- f) I've had enough of your stupid jokes.
- h) She's had four children, and she's expecting a fifth.
- i) Some of these computer games have had a very bad influence on him.

**7**
- a) 's been cutting, hasn't finished
- b) 've been driving
- c) have been playing
- d) 've been saving
- e) have you been going, 've known
- f) 've been looking, haven't found

**8** a) Yet  b) Consequently  c) However
d) Nevertheless  e) As a result

## Listening

**1** The correct order is b), f), a), d), c), g), e).

**2** a) T  b) T  c) F  d) F  e) F  f) F  g) T  h) F

**3** a) craze  b) logging on  c) hooked up to
d) subscribe to  e) check out  f) heading
g) countdown

## Pronunciation

**1** /s/: useful, assumed, fussy, oyster
/z/: visible, civilization, desert, losing, reasonable
/ʃ/: social, delicious, flirtation, mansion, mission

## Vocabulary

**1** a) milk shake  b) soap opera  c) screen addict
d) movie star  e) Beatles album  f) jukebox
g) laptop  h) news media

**2** a) invisibility  b) spaciousness  c) sadness
d) rarity  e) specialty  f) safety  g) difficulty
h) usefulness

**3** a) communication  b) navigation  c) contributions
d) irritation  e) installation  f) flirtation
g) assumption  h) devotion

**4** a) back up  b) browse  c) drag  d) paste  e) install
f) drag  g) paste  h) install  i) browse  j) back up

## Writing

**1** The correct order is d), a), b), c).

**2** a) 3  b) 7  c) 8  d) 1  e) 2  f) 5  g) 10
h) 9  i) 4  j) 6

**3** a) L  b) L  c) E  d) E  e) L  f) L  g) L
h) L  i) E  j) L  k) E  l) E  m) E

---

# 7 Review 1

## Grammar

**1** a) was  b) that/which  c) for  d) the  e) to
f) why  g) being  h) about  i) if  j) would
k) and  l) no/little  m) the  n) made
o) asked/inquired  p) had/wanted

**2** a) been  b) to  c) for  d) it  e) have  f) have
g) the  h) on  i) for  j) to  k) was  l) the

**3**
- a) I was wondering *if/whether* you could spare a minute to help me.
- b) I've *been* having a hard time lately, and I've had enough.
- c) If you had *not* made a mess of your grades in high school, you would have gotten into college.
- d) It's extremely important for us *to* find the right person for the job.
- e) My boss always insists *on* us arriving by eight thirty.
- f) My husband is not interested, and neither *am* I.
- g) Our future depends on whether we can borrow the money we need.
- h) We really don't approve *of* you seeing so much of that man.
- i) When gold was discovered in California, Sutter was already one of *the* wealthiest people in the state.
- j) You won't forget *to* lock the door when you leave, will you?

**4**  a)  had been playing/had played
   b)  being/having been   c) to express
   d)  is always telling   e) hasn't had
   f)  had known   g) would buy
   h)  have been swimming   i) had forgotten
   j)  had become/has become

**5**  a)  He insists on asking embarrassing questions.
   b)  I've been studying economics for three years.
   c)  I was completely taken in by her lies.
   d)  Try not to take it so seriously.
   e)  I'd like to know what time they are going to arrive.
   f)  She is unlikely to object too much.
   g)  We weren't allowed to make any noise.
   h)  If she weren't so talented, she wouldn't have been so successful.

**6**  a) into, back   b) up, at   c) to, on   d) out, down
   e) down, to   f) of, up   g) about, on   h) into, out
   i) on, with

**7**  a) 2   b) 5   c) 7   d) 8   e) 6   f) 1   g) 4   h) 3

## Vocabulary

**1**  a) innocent   b) humiliated   c) urge
   d) entrepreneur   e) breadwinner   f) broke
   g) remedy   h) bouquet   i) aisle   j) bride

**2**  a) notorious   b) useless   c) afford   d) shovel
   e) carbohydrate   f) stuff   g) joke   h) tomb

**3**  a) food   b) line   c) foot   d) hands   e) market   f) neck
   g) legs   h) lunch   i) pride

**4**  a) set   b) make   c) catch   d) do   e) lose
   f) keep   g) see   h) take

**5**  a) balanced diet   b) irreparable damage
   c) job prospects   d) half-baked idea
   e) burning ambition   f) cosmetic surgery
   g) casual look   h) feature film   i) twisted ankle
   j) state championship

**6**  a) perseverance   b) impatient   c) behavior
   d) accidentally   e) annoyance   f) discovery
   g) profitably   h) adaptation   i) convenience
   j) embarrassingly

**7**  a) 3   b) 5   c) 4   d) 6   e) 2   f) 8   g) 1   h) 7